MW00856713

As Long as They're Laughing

As Long as They're Laughing

Groucho Marx
and
You Bet Your Life

by Robert Dwan

Midnight Marquee Press, Inc.
Baltimore, Maryland

Cover Design: Susan Svehla
Frontispiece photo courtesy Paul Wesolowski

Copyright © 2000, Robert Dwan

Without limiting the rights under copyright reserved above, no part of this publication may be reproduced, stored in or introduced into a retrieval system, or transmitted, in any form, or by any means (electronic, mechanical, photocopying, recording, or otherwise), without the prior written permission of the copyright owners or the publishers of the book.

ISBN 1-887664-66-1
Library of Congress Catalog Card Number 105415
Manufactured in the United States of America
First Printing by Midnight Marquee Press, Inc., July 2000

Acknowledgments: Betty Cavanaugh, Photofest, Linda J. Walter, Buddy Weiss, Paul Wesolowski

To John Guedel—
Who invented the whole thing
and Bernie Smith—
Who made it happen

Groucho punches a time clock to celebrate the ninth year (1955) of *You Bet Your Life*. (Courtesy Paul Wesolowski) It wasn't easy to dream up an anniversary photo that made some sense and also earned Groucho's cooperation. It was the job of our head writer, Bernie Smith, and the NBC publicity man, Norman Frisch, and they did it every year for 14 years.

Table of Contents

CBS publicity portrait of Groucho c. 1949 (Courtesy Paul Wesolowski)

As Long As They're Laughing

PREFACE

On the eighth day, God laughed.
—Groucho Marx

Groucho Marx had reached a point of crisis when I met him in 1947. After 40 years in show business, having conquered Vaudeville, Broadway and motion pictures, he found his career at a standstill. He reacted with a series of bold moves that some show business experts thought were foolhardy. He gave notice to Harpo and Chico that he would make no more movies with them, thereby closing the door on the antic world of the Marx Brothers. With that, he deliberately abandoned his unique and long famous theatrical and movie characters, variously named Dr. Hackenbush, Captain Geoffrey T. Spaulding, Rufus T. Firefly, etc., and embraced a new character with a new image to begin a fresh career in an unfamiliar medium.

The unlikely vehicle he chose was a radio quiz show, *You Bet Your Life*. In it he appeared, not in any version of Dr. Hackenbush, not in his private persona of Julius Marx, but as a character combining something of both of them and using the name Groucho.

You Bet Your Life began as a radio program in 1947 on the young and struggling ABC network. In 1949, it was switched to CBS radio, immediately jumped into the ranks of the top 10 programs, and simultaneously received the Peabody award for outstanding achievement in radio. In 1950, the program moved to NBC to begin broadcasting on television while continuing as a simulcast on radio, and Groucho won the Emmy from the TV Academy for "Outstanding TV Personality of 1950." Thereafter, *You Bet Your Life* was consistently among the first two or three programs in the national ratings, and was never out of the top 10. In 1955, almost half of the television sets in America were tuned to Groucho Marx and *You Bet Your Life* each week.

This photo was taken in 1948 after a radio show. I think the man on the right was somebody important, at least he could make Groucho smile. (Courtesy Paul Wesolowski)

Five hundred and twenty-five programs were produced in 14 years for radio and television, in which Groucho encountered 2,500 contestants. The last original program was broadcast on television in June 1961, but *You Bet Your Life* did not die. For four years, there were reruns on NBC-TV. Then, 10 years later, the show was released to syndication and cable and was still being seen as late as 1992.

I was the director of *You Bet Your Life* for its entire run, from its beginning on radio in 1947, through the transition to television, to the close in 1961. John Guedel was the creator and producer of the program, Bernie Smith the head writer. Under Guedel's supervision, Smith and I divided the production responsibilities. Bernie, with a staff of five or six, selected the contestants, prepared the script, and brought the show to the studio. I took it from there, staged the performance, and supervised the editing for broadcast. I did not direct Groucho in any traditional sense. No time limit was placed on the performance of the show. Rather than impose restraints on Groucho, we allowed the performance to run as long as seemed productive. Usually, we filmed about an hour for each half-hour broadcast. It was then my job to edit that 60 minutes, selecting the best material for a 30-minute program.

You Bet Your Life was unique in two respects. Its comedy was based not on actors performing sketch material, but on the personalities and experiences of real people, drawing on their normal lives and occupations. The program's distinction and quality, however, resulted primarily from its giving Groucho Marx an opportunity to exercise his unique skills without the restraints that broadcasting at that time otherwise imposed. Groucho's principal resource was his talent as an improviser of verbal comedy. *You Bet Your Life* was specifically designed to allow him free rein to follow his comic muse, or demon, wherever it led him.

As one of the incidental rewards of working on the show, I had the privilege of participating in a 14-year seminar on comedy with a grand master of the art. Bernie Smith and I had weekly sessions with Groucho as he reviewed the original script, re-wording, approving, rejecting and creating. During the performance, I stood alongside him, just off-camera, as he used the prepared material, re-working it to suit the unpredictable responses of the contestants, adding his own on-the-spot thoughts, inventions and improvisations. He never had to stop and consider whether a remark was beyond the pale of the censorship standards of the time, in bad taste, or just what we called a dirty joke. I did that for him later as his surrogate at the editing stage, exercising the judgment on whether a joke was funny or offensive or worth fighting for with the censor.

In preparing this chronicle, I have been able to draw on some resources not available to anyone else. Through the generosity of John Guedel, I have 20 volumes of the original scripts. As a complement, I have a collection of acetate recordings of the unedited performances and tapes of the edited broadcasts.

A third precious resource is a collection which I inherited from our film editor, Norman Colbert. He bequeathed to me four reels of 16mm film which he had assembled during the 11 years he was the film editor on the program. They consist of the funniest and most audacious of the sequences which we were required to delete from the broadcasts as being unsuitable for viewing in the 1950s. Most of the passages could be broadcast today, and the only eyebrows raised would be Groucho's. But

they furnish documentation of the way standards have changed, not only in American humor, but in other social practices.

Finally, I have drawn on my recollection of our private conversations over a period of almost 20 years. Many of the Groucho remarks that I have reported here have never appeared anywhere else because no one else was present when he said them.

This memoir does not pretend to present an unbiased portrait of Groucho Marx. Obviously, I was an affectionate admirer and devoted disciple. In turn, he respected my position and trusted my judgment. I treasure the remark he made to me, more than once:

> I have nothing but confidence in you. And
> very little of that.

Quintessential Groucho. Perfect construction, perfect timing, an apparently gratuitous compliment, and an immediate retreat from sentimentality. But he meant it, both parts. The confidence, I believe, was real, but so was the implied warning that I'd better deserve it.

In writing this recollection, I have tried to honor Groucho's trust. I have reported what he said to me, what I heard him say to others, what I saw him do.

He did not reveal intimate personal details to me, and I do not pretend to know them. This is an account of a professional relationship through which I propose to give some insight into how Groucho Marx created comedy, and how, for a brief time in his long career, we were able to help him do it.

**Groucho, Zeppo, Chico, Harpo and their father, Sam "Frenchie" Marx c. 1932
(Courtesy Paul Wesolowski)**

As Long As They're Laughing

CHAPTER 1
The Roaches of Nacogdoches

Groucho Marx had been preparing for *You Bet Your Life* all his life, on stage and off. The technique that he perfected during 40 years of constant experimentation involved working within a formal structure—a Vaudeville sketch, a musical comedy script, a motion picture screenplay—and, in performance, creating new material, embellishing, expanding, making changes, substitutions, often improving or at least giving new life to the original material. He had profound respect for the written word, but his basic instinct was to improve any sample of it that fell under his control. He finally became a grand master of the craft of improvisation, a virtuoso practitioner of the art of thinking on his feet.

It began very early, this practice of ad libbing around a core structure. It started in the early Vaudeville act and reached full flower in the 1920s in the Broadway musicals. Finally, in *You Bet Your Life* a vehicle was created especially for Groucho, giving him a scripted structure as a base, with supporting characters as foils, but with complete freedom to ad lib and improvise without restriction.

In the beginning, the Marx Brothers were a musical act, "The Three Nightingales," a vocal trio with Groucho, Gummo, and a girl. Harpo joined, the girl was replaced by a boy who sang bass, and they were "The Four Nightingales." Inevitably, they tried some comedy. Groucho described one of the early efforts in his book, *Groucho And Me:*

> I got a blonde wig. It was an old one my
> mother had discarded. With this, plus a
> market basket with some fake frankfurters
> hanging over the side, I pretended I was
> a German comedian.... The plot consisted
> of me as a butcher boy delivering wieners,

asking Harpo and Gummo (who were dressed as yachtsmen) how to get to Mrs. Schmidt's house. While Gummo pointed me in one direction, Harpo stole the wieners.... This brief, homemade dialogue gave the audience a chance to forget the fact that we had just sung.[1]

In 1907, when they were playing Coney Island, a critic from *Variety,* the holy writ of show business, caught the act, praised the music, but panned the comedy. Minnie Marx, redoubtable mother-manager, forbade any further fooling around between numbers. Comedy was out. You couldn't argue with *Variety.* Or with Minnie.

They were still a musical act two years later as they embarked on a long series of one-night stands on the small-time Vaudeville circuits of the deep South. They were now billed as "The Marx Brothers and Company," Harpo, age 20, Groucho, 18, Gummo, 16, and the "Company," a friend Groucho's age. (Chico, then 21, was temporarily working as a song-plugger, and Zeppo, age 7, was still at home.) They sang their way through Louisiana and into east Texas. In Nacogdoches, Texas, they were appearing in a vacant storefront that qualified as a theater because it had a makeshift platform and some benches. As the boys were singing to a listless audience, a commotion was heard through the front door. In the street outside, a crowd was trying to capture a runaway mule. The entire audience trouped out of the theater to join the chase. The brothers were furious. When the customers returned, the boys let them know how they felt with some pointed remarks about the town and its inhabitants.

"Nacogdoches is full of roaches!" Groucho remembered that line 50 years later.

The audience was caught off guard. There was an ominous silence. Then somebody laughed, and Groucho tried again. There was laughter and applause and a yell for more. The suddenly appreciated performers obliged, threw in a few more songs, and made their exit to the sound of cheers.

In the next town there was no obliging mule, but the troupe looked for chances for comedy in whatever was at hand, before, during and after the songs. It worked. Word spread among the theater managers to watch for a bunch of fresh kids with a funny musical act. A few towns down the road, a manager was waiting. He offered them an extra booking if they would do something special for an audience of teachers in town for a convention. Groucho, recalling a familiar Vaudeville format, put together a school act, "Fun in Hi Skule." Groucho cast himself as Herr Professor, dressed in a frock coat and speaking with a comic German accent. Harpo played Patsy Brannigan, the traditional stupid boy.

PROFESSOR: Vot is the shape of the world?
PATSY: I don't know.
PROFESSOR: Vell, vot shape are my cuff links?
PATSY: Square.
PROFESSOR: Not my veekday cuff links! The vuns I vear on Sundays.
PATSY: Oh, round.
PROFESSOR: All right, vot is the shape of the world?
PATSY: Square on weekdays, round on Sunday!

The teachers of east Texas were delighted, and the Marx Brothers had a new act. Not long after, Chico gave up song plugging and joined his brothers on the road as the irrepressible Italian kid.

The school act was one of the basic Vaudeville formulas. *Variety* counted 62 "Kid Acts" on the Vaudeville circuits as late as 1913. The roots of the form reach deep, even to the classic tradition of the 16th and 17th century Italian comedy troupes, the *commedia dell'arte*, although Groucho would scoff at such pretension. The essential elements of the ancient form were there, however: stock characters, a basic situation or plot and, especially, the freedom to improvise and extemporize within the structure. The Marx Brothers' school act established the basic nature of Groucho's often imitated but essentially inimitable character for the rest of his career. There is a trace of that eccentric authority figure, Herr Professor, in all of his later manifestations, in Professor Quincy Adams Wagstaff, President of Huxley College in *Horse Feathers;* in Rufus T. Firefly, President of the State of Freedonia in *Duck Soup;* in Otis B. Driftwood, the phony impresario in *A Night at the Opera;* and all the others, including even the quizmaster at his lectern in *You Bet Your Life.*

The school act was the beginning of Groucho's career as an improviser. He continued his relentless pursuit of perfection, in the wording of a line, in the timing of a joke, in the definition of his character, as long as he faced an audience.

He describes the process in *Groucho And Me*:

> ...in the old days of Vaudeville... the comedian would steal a few jokes from other acts and find a few in the newspapers and comic magazines.... If the comic was inventive, he would gradually discard the stolen jokes and the ones that died and try out some of his own. In time, if he was any good, he would emerge from the routine character he started with and evolve into a distinct personality of his own. This has been my experience and also that of my brothers.... [2]

The six years following Nacogdoches, from 1909 to 1915, were spent on the road, on Vaudeville circuits all over the country, traveling on trains, battling to improve bookings and billing, working stubbornly to perfect the act. They were hard times. Groucho told me about being stranded without railroad fare in hostile Southern towns and of walking with suitcase in hand to the next one-night stand.

"I think I was in show business 10 years before I had a room with a bath," he said. And in a 1957 interview he said:

> There was nothing romantic about it. It was satisfying, but not enormously so. A Vaudeville actor spent his time in bad hotels and waiting for trains. [3]

He often told me about the sign backstage which carried two admonitions:

> Any act mentioning damn, hell, or God will be canceled without notice. Do not send your laundry out until we have seen your act.

By 1914, the family team was playing bigger towns, with bigger, better theaters. Minnie Marx's brother, Al Shean, of the famous Vaudeville team, "Gallagher and Shean," had written a new act for them. "Home

As Long As They're Laughing

Again" was developed from the original school act, incorporating the best of the new material they had developed on the road.

A major change in the Groucho role came on the evening of May 7, 1915, when the news reached a theater in Toronto that a German submarine had sunk the Lusitania. Herr Professor's German dialect suddenly disappeared, and Groucho became The Teacher, retaining, however, the attitude of eccentric authority.

Now all the elements of the Marx Brothers' act were in place. Harpo had his red wig, and had become a mime. Chico had developed his shoot-the-keys piano technique and his position as a kind of fulcrum, a foil and partner for both Groucho and Harpo. Uncle Al Shean, in writing "Home Again," discovered early what every Marx Brothers' writer found out later. In any dialogue involving Chico, the feed lines had to be just as funny as the responses. That stylistic trick was an essential ingredient in the Marx Brothers formula. The standard Vaudeville comedy team consisted of a straight man and a comic, with feed lines from the straight man, payoffs from the comic. With the Marx Brothers, the roles were not rigidly drawn or even clearly defined. When the going was good, every line got a laugh, Chico's as well as Groucho's. In addition, there were the laughs which sprang from what were not lines at all, but that magical extra ingredient, the pervasive counterpoint of Harpo's pantomime. There were many sequences in which there was no pause between laughs. Theatergoers returned again and again to Marx Brothers shows for two reasons. First, "...the audience was laughing so hard, I couldn't hear the jokes." Second, no two performances were ever exactly alike.

Out of the constant experimentation, out of the ad libbing and fooling around, the flouting of convention and outrageous behavior on and offstage, an identity emerged. In spite of the eccentricity, the act achieved a remarkable level of comic consistency. Groucho said it concisely: "We learned how to get laughs." Finally, eight years after their apprenticeship had started in Coney Island, six years after the epiphany in Nacogdoches, they made it to the top. In 1915, they played the Palace in New York for the first time, and then played it again and again as late as 1930. They were, beyond a doubt, in the big time.

Nevertheless, the next step took eight more years on the road. In 1924, Chico finally found a producer to take them to Broadway. The vehicle was a converted Vaudeville revue called, for no reason, *I'll Say She Is*. The show was greeted with surprised delight by the New York critics and with enthusiastic joy by Broadway audiences. Now, as the quadruple toast of the town, the Marx Brothers were playing in a different league. No need now to ferret out a sugar-daddy producer with an ambitious girlfriend. For their next Broadway show, *The Cocoanuts,* the producer would be Sam Harris, ex-partner of George M. Cohan. No more secondhand music. This time, it was "music by Irving Berlin." And, for this show, there would be no more cobbling together of old Vaudeville routines. *The Cocoanuts* would have an actual book, a real plot, and a definable target for its comedy. It would be written by George S. Kaufman, and it would be a satire on the great Florida real estate boom of the 1920s.

Groucho, especially, was delighted. He had the greatest respect for Kaufman as a writer, and the two men were friends for the rest of their lives. But in 1925, the habits of 18 years in Vaudeville were impossible to break. The script was a wonderful starting point, but all the brothers made their characteristic contributions to the adjustments in the show during the performances. It was a sort of ripening that amounted to metamorphosis as the structure of the book adapted itself to the characters.

Harpo, for instance, invented his blonde-chasing bit in *Cocoanuts* when he persuaded a chorus girl to run screaming across the stage while he pursued her, honking his horn. It happened, perhaps by chance, in the middle of a carefully constructed dialogue between Groucho and Margaret Dumont. Naturally, there was no way to avoid a Groucho comment on the horn-blowing diversion. "First time I ever saw a taxi hail a passenger," was one of his observations.

The blonde-chasing bit stayed in, and so did the additional dialogue by Groucho. In *Animal Crackers,* the next show, also written by George S. Kaufman, this time with Morrie Ryskind, neither Harpo's musical number nor Chico's performance at the piano was in the original script. When Chico's piano spot was inserted in the second act, the brothers developed a complete routine, with commentary by Groucho, including a parody of "The Anvil Chorus" and a football game using Harpo's coat.

Groucho often repeated a remark reported to have been made by George Kaufman during a performance of *Animal Crackers.* Mr. Kaufman was standing in the wings backstage talking to a friend. He interrupted the conversation to listen to the dialogue onstage. Then he turned back to his friend and said:

> Sorry. I was wrong. I thought I just heard
> one of my original lines.

One night in 1960, in Phoenix, Arizona, when we were touring Groucho's play *Time For Elizabeth*, he was standing backstage surrounded by most of the cast and a few friends. He was reminiscing about his days on Broadway:

> I had an understudy when we played *Cocoanuts* on Broadway. He used to sit in the audience every night and try to make notes of the changes. Finally, they had to take him away to an institution.

We all laughed. "No, really," he said. "It's true. He went crazy."

The Marx Brothers conquered Broadway and became the darlings of the New York smart set. Then came Hollywood, and they found their national audience. Starting in 1929, the brothers made movies at the rate of almost one a year. They were uneven, irrational, often inspired, absolutely inimitable. They were wonderful movies, among the funniest ever made, certainly containing some of the funniest scenes ever filmed. They were also vastly successful and profitable.

The practice of constantly working with the written word, seeking perfection, looking for the exact formula to get the laugh, continued even in making the pictures. Part of the process, in the later years, was to take the shows on the road to test the situations and especially the dialogue on a live audience. That was done with *A Night at the Opera* and *A Day at the Races*. Years later, in the late 1970s, George Seaton, director of *A Day at the Races*, reminded Groucho in an interview about their experience with one of the lines in the script, written by the great comedy writer Al Boasberg. Groucho was playing the role of a doctor taking the pulse of a comatose patient. "Is he dead or has my watch stopped?" he asked. The first audience did not laugh. Groucho said,

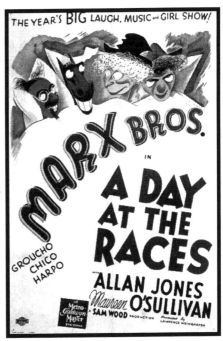

"It's because it's a question, and they're expecting an answer. It should be a statement." The next performance he said, "Either he's dead or my watch has stopped," and the audience yelled.[4]

One cannot help compare that to another of Groucho's medical lines, "Who are you going to trust, me or these crooked x-rays?" It certainly was a successful line and seems to contradict the master's dictum against the interrogative. Perhaps it is an exception because it is a rhetorical question, or because it is so firmly based on his character, or just because it is so damned funny.

Boasberg himself recounted two other examples in a 1987 interview.[5]

> In one scene, Groucho washes his hands in a basin, catches Sig Rumann eyeing his wristwatch, takes it off and throws it in the water. "I'd rather have it rusty than gone," he said, then turned to Boasberg, "Is that the right word?"
>
> It wasn't. Based on 140 stage performances in four cities where they had tried "gone," "disappear" and "missing" nearly 50 times each, the most laughs came from "I'd rather have it rusty than missing."
>
> When Groucho told Chico, "That's the most nauseating proposition I've ever had," they had tried it with "obnoxious," "revolting," "disgusting," "offensive," "repulsive," "disagreeable" and "distasteful."

By 1941 they had made 11 movies in 13 years, and a good deal of the verve had gone out of the process and the product. Groucho, especially, had grown weary of the rigors of movie-making. There must be, he said, an easier way to make a living. There was no economic need for him to work. His investments were under the management of one of the shrewdest and most trustworthy financial advisors in the country, his old friend, Salwyn Shufro. But he was always nervous about the future. Still vivid were memories of the struggle for survival on New York's lower East Side, of the grueling years in small time Vaudeville. Most painful was the memory of that day in October 1929 when his friend, Broadway producer Max Gordon, telephoned to say, "Marx, the jig is up," and

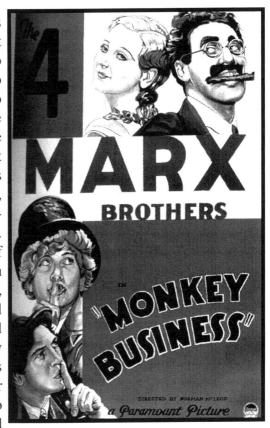

his life savings vanished into the stock market's black hole.

But there was something more than money behind his need to work. He was a performer. Being in show business defined his life. He enjoyed the spotlight, needed an audience. Little as he liked invasions of his privacy, he did treasure the moment when a woman, a total stranger, stopped us on the street and said, "Just keep living, Mr. Marx."

In 1941, Groucho needed a new world to conquer. Vaudeville was gone, comedy clubs did not exist. Night clubs and Las Vegas were not to his taste. He was a superb storyteller in the old tradition of the Vaudeville monologist, but he did not have an act. His oft-quoted witticisms and acerbic comments did not constitute standard one-liners, and, in spite of his reputation as "King Leer," he was not a dirty comic. He did not like the kind of jokes the saloon crowd demanded.

In 1954, in a letter to his daughter Miriam, included in the touching book *Love, Groucho,* he wrote regarding a stag dinner for Leo Durocher. On the dais were Jack Benny, George Jessel, Danny Kaye, Danny Thomas, and George Burns:

I was foolish enough to make a compara-
tively clean speech despite the fact that it
was a stag audience.... However, I have
some kind of a block that doesn't allow me
to shout the customary four-letter words....
I am not amused by the dirty words....[6]

During the war years, of course, he did his share of camp shows,
but that, thank God, was not a permanent solution. Retracing his steps
to Broadway, with or without his brothers, did not attract him, although
he was offered several interesting projects. In February 1945, he wrote
to Miriam:

Kaufman wanted me for the new (Max)
Gordon musical, but they insisted that I
sign up for two years, which means that
if the show clicked, I'd eventually wind
up in Toledo, Chicago and all those other
whistle stops. That's all right when you're
30, but I just couldn't see it, so they got
Moore and Gaxton, I believe.[7]

In 1946, he was offered the title role in a new Theatre Guild production
of *Volpone*, which he rejected for the same reason, and in September
1947, just before *You Bet Your Life* surfaced, he rejected an overture
from Arthur Schwartz and Howard Dietz to play opposite Bea Lillie in
a musical adaptation of John Gunther's book, *Inside USA*. "I intend to
duck all musicals and particularly revues," he wrote to Miriam.[8]

There was a new arena which had developed while the Marxes were
busy making movies. Radio had grown up in the 1930s along with talking
pictures to be the 20th- century replacements for Vaudeville as the domi-
nant forms of popular entertainment. Many of the Vaudeville headliners
were having great success in radio — Fred Allen, Jack Benny, Ed Wynn,
Burns and Allen, Eddie Cantor, Al Jolson, Fanny Brice, Jimmy Durante,
all had become familiar in the American living room.

The Marx Brothers had trouble with radio in the 1930s and '40s.
Harpo, of course, could not adapt at all, and Chico only partially, but
even Groucho, whose character had such a strong verbal base, had limited
success in radio.

As Long As They're Laughing

Groucho's difficulties with radio had multiple causes. First, his basic theatrical role—Geoffrey T. Spaulding, the African explorer in *Animal Crackers,* Professor Quincy Adams Wagstaff, President of Huxley College in *Horse Feathers,* or Dr. Hackenbush in *A Day at the Races*—did not wear well on radio, where the voice alone defined the character. On the stage and the screen his unconventional physical appearance and actions supplied a visual context for the outrageous patterns of his speech. The inappropriate costume, the exaggerated clown-like makeup, the eccentric walk and the impression he gave of inhabiting a slightly different dimension, all contrived to soften the abrasiveness of his verbal assault.

Second, on radio, the classic Marx Brothers trio was reduced to two, lacking the magical visual counterpoint of Harpo. Radio scripts generally eliminated most other supporting cast members, reducing the dialogue to exchanges between Groucho and Chico, with Groucho, naturally, having most of the words.

Finally, Groucho was not able to use his greatest talent, his skill as an improviser. When he did burst the bonds and ad lib, the other actors were distracted because they were all strictly disciplined to stick to the script. In the radio of the 1930s and '40s, network policy insisted that everything be written and submitted in advance to the Continuity Acceptance Department, which, behind the euphemism, was the network censor.

Groucho and Chico made several forays into radio in the early 1930s. They were heard for a season in 1932 in the Marxian lawyer-detective series, *Flywheel, Shyster and Flywheel* for Standard Oil of New Jersey. The show was on at 7:30 p.m. on NBC's minor Blue network, and got a respectable rating. The big hit of the season, however, was Ed Wynn's show on CBS at 9:30, which was playing to an audience twice as large, and to make matters worse, the sponsor was Texaco. Standard Oil canceled after 26 weeks.

In the meantime, the Marx Brothers had other things on their minds. They were suing Paramount over the accounting for *Horse Feathers* and had formed their own production company to make a motion picture of *Of Thee I Sing*. In the end, they returned to Paramount for *Duck Soup*. *Of Thee I Sing* was never made. It is the world's loss that we never saw Groucho as Vice President Alexander Throttlebottom.

In 1934, apparently restless because they weren't making a movie, Groucho and Chico signed with CBS to do a radio show at 7:00 p.m. on Sundays, satirizing the news. Groucho was heard as Ulysses S. Drivel. The program lasted one short season. No matter. They were about to make *A Night at the Opera* for producer Irving Thalberg at MGM, and they were on top of the Hollywood pyramid again.

The Thalberg-produced pictures were different from their previous movies. I have at hand a copy of one of Groucho's rare letters-to-the-editor, written to the *Los Angeles Mirror* in 1961, which gives an insight into some of the thinking behind the Thalberg films *A Night at the Opera* and *A Day at the Races* and, in the last paragraph, gives an explanation for why the team, and especially Groucho, finally stopped making pictures altogether.

A few days before the publication of the letter, the cartoonist Al Capp, then writing a syndicated column, had written a piece in which he stated that when the Marx Brothers switched from anarchistic to semi-lovable humor they lost their audience and had to bow out of pictures.

Groucho wrote:

> Herewith a copy of a letter I have written
> your columnist Al Capp.

Groucho and Chico appear in this publicity still for the 1932-33 radio series *Flywheel, Shyster & Flywheel.* **(Courtesy Paul Wesolowski)**

"If I were not an ardent admirer of your works, I wouldn't go to all this trouble to explain a few things about the facts of life to you.

"I am in complete accord with what you wrote about Mr. Nixon's lack of lovability contributing to his defeat. However, when you write about the Marx Brothers, like most other columnists, you don't know what the hell you are talking about.

"The reason we switched from being anarchistic in our humor to being semilovable was simply a matter of money. In our early pictures, we were, as you said, hilariously funny fellows, knocking over the social mores and customs of our times, but with each succeeding picture the receipts slipped just a bit.

"Our last anarchistic (to use your description) picture was *Duck Soup*. We then signed with Irving Thalberg, who said, 'Of course I want you fellows to continue to be funny, but if somewhere in the story you occasionally help someone, the audiences will like you better and your pictures will be financially more successful.' *Duck Soup* grossed $1,250,000, while *A Night at the Opera*, our first picture for Thalberg (made under the sign of lovability), grossed close to $5,000,000.

"In conclusion, our audiences didn't drop us. We dropped them. The pictures became physically too tough to do and we decided to retire to greener and more comfortable pastures."
Groucho Marx
NBC Studios
Sunset and Vine
Hollywood.

In the early 1940s, the radio appearances included a fairly steady schedule of bookings on *The Dinah Shore Show* and scattered guest shots — *Hollywood Hotel* in 1937, *The Bob Hope Show* in 1938, an all-star salute to President Roosevelt in 1940, and sporadic bookings with Rudy Vallee and Frank Sinatra. And there were frequent appearances on the Armed Forces Radio Shows, *Mail Call* and *Command Performance*, broadcast to troops still overseas.

There were some problems for Groucho in these shows. In October 1945, he wrote to Miriam:

> ...I have very little control over the quality of the material. I don't have the advantage of [Fred] Allen or [Jack] Benny or any of the other comics who are permanent fixtures and work their way all through a script and can rely on events that happened in their shows previously for laughs. I have to go to bat from scratch each time I appear.[9]

In 1939, he participated in one of the rare experimental programs in the history of commercial radio. It was called *The Circle*, and the permanent cast included Ronald Colman, Laurence Tibbett, Madeleine Carroll, Cary Grant, Carole Lombard, Basil Rathbone, and Chico and Groucho Marx. Among other things, Groucho had a chance to do some delightful domestic sketches with Madeleine Carroll. The program was sometimes brilliant and occasionally contentious backstage. Once Groucho and Chico expanded a six-minute spot to 11 minutes, and Basil Rathbone declared he was quitting because of Groucho's ad-libbing.[10] The program was canceled before Rathbone could fulfill his threat.

By that time, especially after the death of Irving Thalberg, neither picture-making nor the pictures produced were as much fun anymore, and there was a long hiatus after *The Big Store* in 1941. Groucho was available for radio, but there were no takers. In 1943, he did have his own program, *Pabst Blue Ribbon Town*, in which he and a troupe toured military camps with a variety show. After a run of 46 weeks, Groucho was replaced by Danny Kaye. It was a bitter blow.

In October 1946, he wrote to Miriam.

> I must tell you that I may be involved in another radio show before the year ends. Perhaps even with Mickey Rooney. That's

a nice, pleasant thought to toy with. I have given up being a success on the air. The way I figure it out, I just have too much talent for it; it requires a mediocrity that I can't acquire.... So now I grab what money I can and know that in a few months the sponsor will listen one day, and there goes Groucho Marx. I figured it up, and despite the fact that I have never been a success on the air, I have played over two hundred weeks in a matter of five years....[11]

Meanwhile, his friend, screenwriter Irving Brecher, had developed an idea for a series called *The Flotsam Family*, in which Groucho would play an average citizen beset by the problems of domestic life. It was a good idea and they produced a funny script, but they couldn't sell it with Groucho in the lead. In disgust, Groucho gave his rights in the property to Brecher. A short time later, with Groucho's approval, Brecher rewrote the script, changed the character to an Irishman, and sold the show under the title, *The Life of Riley*. It had a long run on radio and television starring William Bendix, and a shorter time on television with Jackie Gleason.

There was one other notable radio performance by Groucho, in 1945, in a truly extraordinary production of *The Undecided Molecule*, written and directed by Norman Corwin. It epitomized Corwin's "theatre of the mind" in managing to define the precious uniqueness of humanity in words and sounds and music. Groucho played the pivotal role of the Judge in a cast which included Robert Benchley, Vincent Price, Sylvia Sidney, and Keenan Wynn.

In 1946, Groucho was persuaded to appear in one more movie with his brothers, *A Night in Casablanca*. The best result of that venture is a series of letters Groucho wrote to the Warner Bros.' legal department contesting their claim to exclusive rights to the name "Casablanca." Groucho countered by challenging the Warners' right to the word "Brothers," to Jack Warner's right to "Jack," Harry's right to "Harry," and the corporation's right to Luther Burbank's name for its studio. For the complete text of the classic letters, I refer you to *The Groucho Letters* published by Simon and Shuster in 1967.

A Night in Casablanca had one other significant consequence. It permanently soured Groucho on the business of movie-making. He often recounted the moment of truth. It came at one o'clock in the morning at the desperate end of a day's shooting on a cavernous sound stage at the General Service Studios in Hollywood. Hanging upside-down by his knees from a ladder extending from a fake airplane, being blasted by a wind machine simulating a 100-mile-an-hour airstream, Groucho thought, "This is no way for a man my age to make a living." He told his brothers that *A Night In Casablanca* would be their last picture together. He was retiring from the motion picture business.

The time had come for *You Bet Your Life*.

Groucho and Bob Hope in 1946, backstage after an all-star radio special. Onstage a short time earlier they had both dropped their scripts and adlibbed a few minutes. The incident led, eventually, to *You Bet Your Life*. (Courtesy Paul Wesolowski)

CHAPTER 2
Julius and Groucho

Bob Hope was onstage in a Hollywood radio studio one spring evening in 1946 as master of ceremonies for a star-studded special designed to advertise a One-Cent Sale for Walgreen Drug Stores. The show was running long, and Groucho Marx was pacing impatiently in a drafty hallway, long past his scheduled time. Finally the moment came for Groucho's entrance. Bob Hope, supposedly stranded in the desert, delivered the prototypical radio entrance cue, "Why, Groucho Marx, what are you doing out here in the middle of the Sahara Desert?"

"Sahara Desert, hell!" Groucho said. "I've been freezing out in the hallway for 45 minutes!"

Hope, by accident or design, dropped his script, Groucho politely followed suit, and they proceeded to ad lib until the frantic producers sent someone out to pick up the scripts.

Witness to this historic event was John Guedel, who was there with his partner, Art Linkletter, to stage a segment inspired by their popular show, *People Are Funny*. John Guedel's realm was the world of audience participation programs, game shows, quiz shows, anything in which you used real people instead of hiring actors. In his youth, he had invented the singing commercial. At 32, Guedel was producer of *People Are Funny* on NBC radio and *House Party*, a daytime radio program airing five times a week on CBS. Later, when he and television were blooming together, Guedel had 18 half-hour programs on national networks every week.

After the show, Guedel approached Groucho and remarked that no radio program had ever taken advantage of Groucho's ability to ad lib. Why didn't they plan a show in which he could do just that? What kind of a show? A quiz show. Groucho did not immediately embrace the notion.

A quizmaster then, and in most cases now, was merely expected to read questions and answers from a paper and keep score, while encouraging extravagant enthusiasm in the contestants. It did not seem a suitable role for the toast of Broadway, the movie star, and darling of the literati. *Newsweek* later said it was like selling champion race horse Citation to a glue factory. In spite of not having a regular program, Groucho was not exactly idle. There were frequent guest appearances and other activities. On October 2, 1947, he wrote to his daughter Miriam:

> Sunday, Kay [his new young wife] and I are flying to Frisco to play five hospitals in three days, and then when I come back I am doing an air show for the boys overseas... and an appearance at an orphan asylum.[1]

But he didn't have a regular show, and he had a real need to keep occupied. In May 1956, he wrote to Miriam just after he had finished writing a magazine article:

> It isn't the money particularly that I write for, it's just that I am a restless soul and when I am not working I get too introspective and that only leads to unhappiness. I am afraid I will always have to have some work to keep me from thinking too much about myself and the state of the union and the world.[2]

So, when John Guedel proposed the quiz show, Groucho finally agreed, but with negligible enthusiasm. He wrote to Miriam:

> This is my last fling on the air. If I don't click this time, I will be convinced it is not the medium for me, and confine my waning talents to other fields.[3]

He and Guedel each invested $125 to make a sample recording.

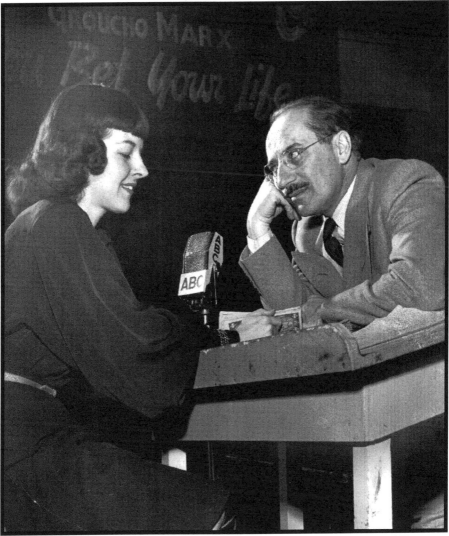

A publicity photo taken after an ABC radio performance in 1947. The obligatory pretty girl is probably a winning contestant. (Courtesy Paul Wesolowski) You can tell how fancy the set for the radio show was by the condition of the table.

On October 18, after he had recorded several programs, but a week before the first broadcast, his mood was still of cautious optimism, or as optimistic as he ever got:

> Frankly, I don't see why the quiz show should create any furor, it's just another one, there are a hundred on the air, and

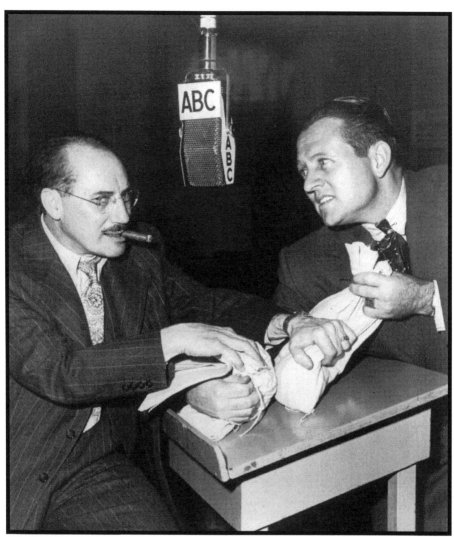

John Guedel was producer of Art Linkletter's *People Are Funny, House Party,* and Groucho's *You Bet Your Life.* Both were partners with Guedel and here, as a joke, Groucho and Art are posed haggling over the profits. (Courtesy Paul Wesolowski)

they all give away money.... But I love radio. If the show clicks, it's better than any kind of show business. Particularly for a man of my years. It means no getting up early in the morning and making up and memorizing and all the physical discomforts that the rest of the business presents. So I am going to work hard at it and try and do it as well as I can, and not insult anybody that is connected with the show in any way.[4]

The pilot radio program was recorded in a CBS studio using the Linkletter *House Party* audience. John took the recording to all three networks, but even with Groucho's name and John's track record, no one was interested. But Guedel was not one to be stopped by the conventions of the market place. He read in *Daily Variety* that Allan Gellman, President of the Elgin American Company, was in Hollywood looking for a program to advertise their compacts, cigarette cases and dresser sets. Elgin American had never sponsored a radio program, but Gellman had seen Groucho in *Animal Crackers* on Broadway and thought he was funny. He bought *You Bet Your Life* and a weekly half hour of time on ABC, the least expensive of the networks, to start Monday, October 27, 1947. By December 12, Groucho was able to write to Miriam:

I am having the time of my life doing this show. I like the radio, and what is just as important is that all my friends seem to think I have found my métier at last in this business. They all like the show and that gives me a glow....[5]

The glow continued. On January 3, 1948 he wrote:

...out here it is a veritable sensation. As you know, I was embarrassed about doing a quiz show, for it is considered the lowest form of radio life, but all of my friends, the ones who make big salaries and listen to *Information, Please* and the other erudite programs, are nuts about this. I just don't understand it, but apparently the quality of ad-libbing on the air is so low that if anyone comes along with even a moderately fresh note he's considered practically a genius. Don't be surprised, but I think your old man has finally arrived in radio. You could knock me over with a microphone.[6]

He continued to enjoy doing the show all during its run. In January 1950, he gave an interview to *Time* magazine when we moved into television.

> In the old days they almost threw me off the air if I deviated from the script. I had to sign a written pledge that I would read only what was before me. But now I'm doing what comes naturally. It's like stealing money to get paid for this.[7]

To head the writing staff for the pilot and the series, John brought in Bernie Smith, former San Diego newspaper man and *People Are Funny* writer, who was then producing the West Coast portion of the *We the People* radio program. I was a staff writer-director for NBC in Hollywood and was moonlighting as a writer for Guedel and Linkletter on *People Are Funny*. When John offered me the job as director on the new Groucho Marx radio show, I decided to quit the staff job at NBC. I seemed to be trading security for very little more money. It was a good decision. Even so, I kept the writing job on *People Are Funny* as a hedge until *You Bet Your Life* went on television three years later.

On *You Bet Your Life*, the first item on the agenda was what character Groucho would play. Obviously, since it was radio at the start, there was no problem with the visual image — no frock coat, no painted mustache. But how would he play him, this quizmaster? The decision was made, I believe, without great deliberation. Groucho knew how he wanted to play him, as himself, simply as Groucho. Groucho himself, however, is not a simple character. There is, first of all, the private person, who I think of most often as Julius, although I never called him that. His old friend, George Jessel, was the only one I know of who called him Julius. His older children called him Padre. Melinda, while I knew her, called him Daddy. His wives called him Groucho, or, sometimes, though not usually pejoratively, Grouch. His close friend and sometime writing collaborator, the playwright Norman Krasna, called him Hackenbush.

When Julius was in ascendance, he was soft-spoken, thoughtful, even gentle. When Groucho was in control, he was the realist, the wit, the

**Zeppo, Groucho, Chico, Gummo and Harpo in 1938. (Courtesy Paul Wesolowski)
Gummo was the troupe's business manager, but everyone usually took part in
negotiations, especially Groucho and Chico.**

iconoclast. It was really quite a remarkable feat that Julius Marx accomplished, one that few men have been able to do. He invented a character who was accepted by society as a legitimate gadfly, who could lash out with impunity at individual or organized stupidity. It was his accepted role to search for the cracks in the veneer of polite convention and by applying pressure at the weak points, perhaps reveal some vein of truth.

Beyond that, there was a sort of Super-Groucho, outrageous, sometimes vulgar, sometimes cruel, a role he played in public "because they'd be disappointed if I didn't insult them." The earliest recorded instance of the Super-Groucho occurred when he was about 14 years old. He and Harpo attended a performance by the great Harry Houdini. The boys sat in the front row, and Houdini called them onstage. He was about to do his famous trick in which he pulled an endless string of threaded needles from his mouth, and he wanted someone to testify that he had nothing hidden there.

Groucho poses for this 1930s publicity shot. (Courtesy Paul Wesolowski)

"I want you to look in my mouth and tell the audience what you see." Houdini opened wide, and one of the young men looked.

"What did you see?" Houdini asked.

"Pyorrhea," young Julius said.

Houdini threw them off the stage.

The conviction that he was somehow entitled to say anything with impunity stayed with him the rest of his life. In 1958, on vacation in Paris, we were strolling on the embankment along the river Seine when he decided to try the only French phrase he knew. He stopped a very smartly dressed woman and said, "*Voulez-vous coucher avec moi?*" She stared at him with a mixture of incomprehension and disbelief and then went on her way. He tried it once more, but, I presume, his abominable French accent saved him from repercussions.

One time in Romanoff's restaurant in Hollywood, a man asked to shake his hand. Groucho obliged.

"You'll never know how much this means to me," the man said.

"To me, it probably means a skin disease," Groucho replied.

A few minutes later, the man was happily quoting the remark to his friends.[8] Most of the time, such sallies were received without resentment. To be insulted by Groucho Marx was generally considered a mark of distinction, certainly grist for the small-talk circuit.

Groucho did, in fact, privately revel in his self-bestowed freedom of speech. He often told of being invited to a studio preview of the spectacle, *Samson and Delilah,* produced by Cecil B. DeMille and starring Hedy Lamarr and Victor Mature. After the showing, DeMille asked him for his opinion.

"I don't think the picture will be a success," Groucho said. "The leading man has bigger tits than the leading lady."

Once in New York, in the Plaza Hotel, a priest said, "My mother is crazy about you." Groucho said, "I didn't know you fellows had mothers. I thought it was immaculate conception."

Later that same evening, in Sardi's, two people stopped by his table. "We're from Alabama, and we just love your show." Groucho didn't pause. "Well, see that the Negroes get the vote." They froze momentarily, then laughed and moved on.

In Las Vegas, Ken Murray was talking to Groucho backstage after Murray's show. Murray was complaining. "I have trouble sleeping."

"Have you ever tried sitting in your audience?" Groucho asked. Murray spent the rest of the evening telling everyone what Groucho had said.

Most of the time, it was a kind of automatic reflex. In 1948 on *You Bet Your Life*, he was talking to Mrs. Mary Paternick.

MRS. PATERNICK:	When I was young....
GROUCHO:	You're still young, Mrs. Paternick.
MRS. PATERNICK:	Oh I wouldn't say that!
GROUCHO:	I wouldn't say it either, but I'm supposed to be nice to you.

Anyone close to him was likely to be the recipient of one of those barbs. I was not immune. A friend of mine, the writer Ralph Schoenstein, sent me a page from the *New Yorker* which contained his by-line on a short story and a cartoon by William Hamilton about the Marx Brothers. It showed a college seminar in which a student was saying, "The tautology of their symbolism thus begins to achieve mythic proportions in *A Day at the Races, Duck Soup* and *A Night at the Opera*." Ralph autographed the page: "To Bob, a man I like to remember, Ralph." I showed it to Groucho and asked him to autograph it to me. He obliged: "To Bob, a man to forget, Groucho."

The insult, in fact, has unfortunately become almost a definition of Groucho. The only entry under his name in the 14th edition of *Bartlett's Quotations* is: "I never forget a face, but in your case I'll make an exception."[9]

In practice, though, the three aspects of his personality melded and intertwined, changing modes with no perceptible strain. I remember an occasion when we were at the Arizona Biltmore, on a trip making television commercials for our sponsor, DeSoto. The episode started with Julius in the ascendancy. We had entered the dining room and been stopped near the door by a man who owned a string of winning horses and several counties in California.

"Harpo!" he boomed. "I want you to meet my friend Phoebe. My dear, this is Harpo."

Mr. Marx politely acknowledged the introduction. As he moved away, I said, "It's nice to be recognized wherever you go, Harpo."

"I didn't want to embarrass him," Julius replied.

Almost immediately, the spirit of Groucho returned. The dining room was a huge formal space with high ceilings and thick carpets bordering on an enormous dance floor. On the far side, where traditionally aproned waitresses fluttered in the background, Groucho's wife and daughter were seated at a table waiting. As we approached the edge of the dance floor, Groucho held out his arms. "Shall we dance?" he asked. And we did, in the antic spirit of the Marx Brothers, alternately leading and following in a swooping Viennese waltz, ending at the table with deep, formal bows. Mrs. Marx, not in the least surprised, said nothing. Melinda said, "Oh, Daddy!"

Our waitress was not young, but she was pleasant. "Did anyone ever tell you that you look like Greer Garson?" Julius was speaking again.

"Oh, come now!" She did not really believe him, but she knew he was not making fun of her.

A nine-year-old boy appeared, planted himself firmly against Mr. Marx's shoulder, and placed a menu between his spoon and the soup. "Autograph," he demanded. A beaming mother appeared with a silver pen. "Freddy watches your show every week," she said. Groucho resurfaced.

"You ought to be ashamed of yourself," he said. "Why isn't he in bed where he belongs? You'd better keep an eye on that boy. He's a potential juvenile delinquent." Mother and son left happily. Groucho had not disappointed their expectations.

The quizmaster on *You Bet Your Life*, when full flower was reached, was basically Groucho, with occasional flashes of Julius and frequent forays into the realm of the convention-defying Super-Groucho.

There was the gentle voice of Julius, shifting into a Groucho construction, in his reply to a pretty young woman who had told him she had gone to a beauty parlor before her first date with her husband.

GROUCHO: That was coals to Newcastle, Marjorie. You didn't have to do that.

MARJORIE: Oh, I'm afraid you're a flatterer!

GROUCHO: I am, but you don't have to be afraid.

Super-Groucho grabbed the reins when an Idaho farmer assured him that potatoes, by themselves, were not fattening.

"You put sour cream and butter on a mattress, and it'll be fattening," the gentleman from Idaho said.

"That's the only thing I haven't had on a mattress," Super-Groucho replied.

So Groucho was Groucho in all his aspects on radio, with very little difference between his behavior offstage and on.

And when the time came to move to television in 1950, Groucho, strongly supported by Guedel, insisted on remaining Groucho. It was the opinion of all the instant experts that he was squandering a great resource. Television is a visual medium, they said, and Dr. Hackenbush with painted eyebrows and mustache, frock coat and loping walk was made-to-order. A television show must have action, production numbers, dancing girls. The model was Milton Berle's wildly successful *Texaco*

Star Theater in which Uncle Miltie tried every trick known to Vaudeville and burlesque, with the criterion, apparently, that something always be moving across the screen.

Groucho disagreed. If millions of people had enjoyed listening on radio to one man perched on a stool, they would enjoy watching him and his guests on television. Otherwise, the maestro said, we had no show, and making an entrance in a sedan chair would not make any difference. (In 1961, we did have him make his entrance through the audience in *Animal Crackers* style, in a sedan chair borne by four Screen Extras Guild natives. It didn't make any difference. We were off the air the next year, anyway.)

So, the character stayed Groucho and did not revert to Hackenbush. When Bernie Smith said to him, "You have to wear the painted mustache and the frock coat," Groucho replied, "The hell I will. That character's dead!"

In a review of Maxine Marx's book *Growing Up With Chico*, Walter Kerr, the distinguished *New York Times* drama critic, defined the impact of the Groucho-Hackenbush character on a movie audience:

> We may admire Groucho, but we can't possibly cope with him. His headlong assault—very often into the camera, at us—is so overwhelming that our collapse into helpless laughter is really a form of self-defense. [10]

It would have been too much for weekly exposure on television. It could not have worked as a medium for relating to six total strangers each week. As a result of Groucho's insight and determination, the eyebrows stayed natural, he wore a bow tie and a sport coat—the same one every week to allow for flexibility in editing. (It was specially designed to look good when he was sitting down—the only jacket in television that did not wrinkle behind the neck when the wearer was seated.) He did make one concession. Bernie persuaded him that most people pictured him as wearing a mustache, so he grew a real one.

After the first TV broadcast, some critics complained that it was not a television show because it had no action. The rebuttal came from Groucho's friend, Goodman Ace, in his column in *The Saturday Review of Literature,* October 28, 1950:

(Courtesy Paul Wesolowski)

...and then came the first Groucho
Marx show on television.... Here was a
man with a new theory.... He conceded
nothing to television but what he had
to say.

Jack Gould, Radio and Television
Editor for the *New York Times*, stated

(Photofest)

As Long As They're Laughing

when one of the quiz contestants made some readily misunderstandable answer to Groucho's brassy questioning....

[But] Ben Gross, in his column in the *Daily News*... was displeased with the Marx show. "This is not TV," he said.... "This is radio." Later in the week, this same opinion on sight and sound appeared... in *Variety*...

This essay does not advocate the abolishment of action in television.... [But] there are shows which can be just as entertaining if a man sits there quietly smoking a cigar and leering through his moustache.... Oh, yes, he gave them action. He moved his lips, and bright, adult sounds came out.[11]

Now it is 1958 and for the 11th time we need an anniversary photo. Groucho obliges by wearing his Captain Spaulding pith helmet. The duck head and carnival wheel are imitations of the actual ones used on the show that year. (Courtesy Paul Wesolowski)

CHAPTER 3
You Bet Your Life

The format of *You Bet Your Life* was simple. In performance, three pairs of contestants appeared to engage in conversation with Groucho and then play a quiz game. The rules of the game varied from season to season, but typically the players were given a small stake to bet on a series of three or four questions. The amount of money in that preliminary round was always modest, usually starting with $20, which could be run up to $160. The players winning the most money were entitled to try "the big question" at the end of the program. The bounty here was relatively small, too, compared to the big-money programs of the era, such as the *$64,000 Question*. We started with a $1,000 jackpot which increased by $500 each week the question was missed. It was an occasion for fanfare and portentous announcement when our big money reached as much as $3,000.

You Bet Your Life was a comedy program, and the comedy between Groucho and the guests was the indispensable element. Nevertheless, the quiz was an essential ingredient. It immediately removed us from the realm of sketch comedy. The players were there for the stated purpose of winning some money in the quiz. They were not performers setting out to be funny.

As for the other trappings of the standard television spectacle, we were saved by our minuscule budget. There was no appropriation for dancing girls, not even for a smiling curvaceous assistant to usher in the contestants, and no one had yet thought of electronic scoreboards. George Fenneman would continue to do the smiling, the ushering, and the scorekeeping.

After three years on radio, Bernie Smith wrote a very good script for the first television show, involving a move to a second set for the quiz and a pretty girl at a cashier's window to pay the money. It was never used.

There was no room in the budget for an elaborate new set. There was no room in the budget for any set. Our appropriation for sets on the first TV show was the same as it had been for radio: zero. We had performed the radio show in front of the studio drape, why not do the TV shows the same way? No reason, except that the drape was a peculiar dark green color that appeared muddy black on film. After the third telecast, BBDO, the advertising agency for our new sponsor, the DeSoto-Plymouth Dealers, flew a vice-president out from New York to deliver his expert opinion, and NBC reluctantly pulled a drape of a different color out of its storehouse.

Today, the program is often identified as "the show with the duck," referring to the stuffed bird which appeared when one of our guests said the secret word and won an extra $100. That elaborate nonsense was characteristic of a John Guedel production. Guedel liked to have something happen that was anticipated but unpredictable. On *People Are Funny*, he sometimes had Art Linkletter announce that an alarm clock had been set to go off at a randomly selected time. The person talking at that moment would receive a prize. For *You Bet Your Life,* John invented the secret word. At the beginning of the program, out of earshot of potential contestants, George Fenneman, in his most sonorous tones, would say:

> Ladies and gentlemen, the secret word
> tonight is spoon, S-P-O-O-N. You Bet
> Your Life!

And the show was under way.

On the radio program, when anyone said the secret word, no matter where it was in the conversation, a fire bell would ring, and the orchestra would play a triple-time version of "The Stars and Stripes" or, later, "Hooray for Captain Spaulding." When we went on television, our team of creative geniuses struggled with the problem of inventing some interesting visual device that could appear and disappear without leaving a trace and, most important, would not cost any money. The duck did not appear until the 10th TV show. Various makeshift schemes were tried. On the seventh TV show, for instance, George Fenneman opened his coat to reveal a placard strapped to his waist. Finally, Bernie Smith said to Groucho that it ought to be some kind of a bird, maybe a chicken. "A duck," Groucho said. "Ducks are funny." Bernie designed and constructed the duck in his

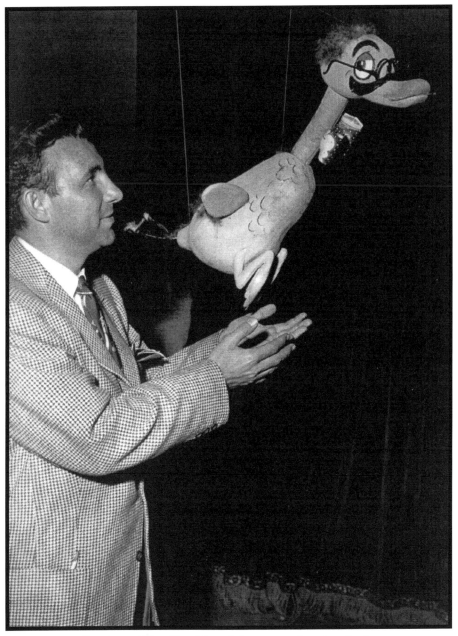

Producer John Guedel and the money-bearing duck.

garage. Groucho was right. It was a funny duck, and a fairly disrespect-
ful caricature of Groucho—glasses, painted eyebrows and mustache,
bow tie on a scrawny neck. It bore a placard in its beak identifying the
secret word and two $50 bills tucked behind its anatomically incorrect

This publicity photo is captioned, "Fowl or Fair? Bomb-toting duck fights back quickly (and quackly) after Groucho Marx replaces him with Marilyn Burtis, a slick chick as the "secret word" paying teller who flies through the air on NBC's radio and TV *You Bet Your Life*. Only one can survive—which will it be?" (4/18/56) Pretty as she was she only lasted one show. (Photofest)

knees to pay the contestants. Its operation on the show was as primitive as possible. It was suspended on piano wire, which we made no effort to conceal, and operated by a stage hand who was required to stay at his post, on the ready, during the entire 80-minute filming session. Several years later, when we had a little money in the budget, I introduced some variations, ranging from a papier-mâché, multi-armed, Hindu god to a man in a gorilla suit and a pretty girl on a swing. Nothing worked as well as the duck.

On one of our earliest broadcasts, George Fenneman opened the show by identifying the secret word and continuing with the usual statement:

> If anyone says the secret word during the
> next half hour, he wins $250.

Immediately after that broadcast, the NBC operators in New York received a phone call from an alert listener in New Jersey who stated that he had said the word "face" during the previous half hour and demanded his $250. The next week, we changed the statement to read:

> If any of our *contestants* says the secret
> word, he wins $250.

The amount, under later budgets, was reduced to $100.

Although Bernie Smith never admitted it to me, I am convinced from the circumstantial evidence that he did, on occasion, rig the secret word to make sure that some worthy contestant won some money, even if he should go broke in the quiz. One evening near Christmas time in 1948, our radio guests were a Mr. and Mrs. Healey, who had nine children. She was asked about Christmas traditions in her house. She said the kids liked the toy Santa Claus with a music box on its back. The music box, she said, played "Jingle Bells," and, by coincidence, the

The figure whose teeth Groucho is testing is a man in a gorilla suit who replaced the duck for one week—one week only! (Photofest)

Bernie Smith, head writer and my partner during the entire run of *You Bet Your Life*, *Tell It to Groucho*, and *Groucho in Britain*. In spite of the somber expression he was a pretty funny guy.

secret word that night was "bells." Bernie had written the script, knew the question and her answer, and, I am sure, picked the word to do the job. She had been asked in her preliminary interview what she would do with the money if she should win it. Her reply, which she fortunately remembered to repeat on the show, was, "I'd like to take all nine kids to a shoe store and get all nine new shoes at the same time for once." It was all in a good cause.

You Bet Your Life was never broadcast directly as performed. It was always recorded or taped for radio and filmed—never videotaped—for television. Until three days before the first radio broadcast, however, the program was scheduled to be aired live. I had always assumed that some-one at ABC or at the agency or sponsor had suddenly become nervous about allowing Groucho free rein on the airways with no protection of script or recording. John Guedel recently told me what actually happened. The credit goes to Bing Crosby, although I'm sure he never knew it.

In 1947, there was a rule in force at all three networks against the broadcast of recorded programs. It would lower the standards of qual-ity, the engineers insisted. There were some exceptions. Because of the three-hour time difference between the East and the West, programs like *The Bell Telephone Hour of Fine Music* originating in New York at 8 p.m. and arriving on the Pacific Coast at 5 p.m., were recorded for later broadcast to the Western states. The other exception was the *Bing Crosby Show* on ABC. Crosby, who was pretty well king of the ABC mountain, had persuaded the network in 1946 to let him record his program. He wanted the safeguard of being able to do a second take on a song, of correcting a gaffe or a blooper, or of improving the quality of the sound by electronic means. When Groucho signed to go on ABC, John Guedel was in the network offices the next morning. If Crosby could record, why not Groucho? He did not tell the network the real reason for his anxiety. He was not worried about scandalous or libelous or dirty material. He was afraid that Groucho might get so entranced with talking to the guests and telling old Vaudeville jokes that he would never get around to play-ing the quiz game, which at that juncture promised to be the heart of the program.

We recorded the first show on acetate records (because audiotape did not exist) three days before it was scheduled to be broadcast. Designed to be a 30-minute program, the performance lasted approximately an hour. Dorothy Nye, John's valiant secretary, made a typed transcript from the recording, John listened to the replay, marked the transcript to indicate what he thought should be deleted, and gave it to me to edit. Fine. But how do you cut a phonograph record?

I had one clue. During World War II, the Armed Forces Radio Service had taken the big network radio shows — Jack Benny, Charlie McCarthy, Bob Hope — and removed the commercials for release of the programs to the troops in the camps and overseas. They did this by using several copies of the same show and re-recording the entertainment portions, skipping the commercials.

You Bet Your Life was a bit more complicated. We wanted to remove single words and phrases as well as paragraphs. There was an audience in the background, laughing most of the time, and a host who rarely waited for anyone else to finish speaking before he spoke. It was impossible, but we did it. Or, rather, Hal Lee did it while I watched. Hal was an NBC recording engineer with an impeccable ear, unflagging spirits, and the skills of an acrobatic dancer. He met our impossible demands 36 weeks in a row. And almost no one knew that the program was edited. Our aim, on both radio and television, was to make the show sound as if it were being broadcast live, as if Groucho were just sitting there baffling the contestants in real time.

After that first harrowing year of editing acetate recordings, we received a wondrous gift—facilities for recording and editing on magnetic tape. Once again, Bing Crosby played a role. The story starts with an engineer named Jack Mullin who had returned from Germany after the war with a Magnetophone, the first professional high fidelity tape recorder. Mullin rebuilt the machine, redesigning the electronics, and attracted the attention of Ampex, a small company looking for a postwar product. They joined forces to produce the first Ampex tape recording machine and start the American tape recording industry.

In Hollywood, the technical producer for Bing Crosby's ABC radio program, Murdo MacKenzie, a man with integrity and determination to match his name, heard a demonstration of the first Ampex recorders and persuaded Crosby to listen to a tape. Bing immediately called ABC and proposed that the network buy some of the equipment. A suggestion from Crosby at that time was the equivalent of a royal command, especially at struggling ABC. They investigated Ampex, but concluded that they needed some guarantee of continued production from the tiny company before making a major investment in its equipment. Crosby sent Ampex an unsolicited check for $50,000, and Ampex was suddenly off and running. Three editing machines came to Hollywood, two for the Crosby show and one for *You Bet Your Life* radio. It was all we needed.

That early Ampex machine was a delight for doing our kind of editing. It recorded at the speed of 30 inches of tape per second, so that the slightest pause in the dialogue extended over several inches of tape, and we could sometimes slip a razor blade in between syllables.

As recording engineer and tape editor, I had the help of Molly, a tall, slender, beautiful young woman whose last name is unfortunately lost in the mists of my memory. Molly and I learned together how to do magnetic tape editing. One of our limitations was that we had only one tape machine. To delete material in a comedy soundtrack—to remove a joke that didn't work or to excise some dialogue that had been censored—it was often possible to fade out of one laugh and fade back into another laugh that had occurred several seconds later in performance, skipping the material in-between. If it was done skillfully, using two tapes and fading from one tape machine to a second, the deletion could not be detected. But we had only one machine, so we had to invent an alternative method. Molly did it by physically cutting the tape on a long bias. She placed the two strips of tape containing the two laughs on top of each other and, using a razor blade, cut them in half on the bias, so that when they were pasted back together they faded into one another and the joke that had been in between was deleted. Because of the fast speed of the machine, the splice was often three feet long. I don't believe anyone else ever employed such a device.

When the time came to make the transition to television, again, there were no clues. Nobody had ever tried to do what we wanted to do.

As director, my biggest challenge was to translate the easy-going, relaxed radio show into an equally tension-free television production. First, Groucho must be free to improvise, as on radio, with the same confidence that recording and editing were in place as his safety net. In 1950, videotape was not available for broadcasting—motion picture film was the only solution. Also no color television existed, so black and white film was the only choice. This was fortunate, because if we had been forced to shoot in color, our film cost would have been prohibitive.

Our second imperative was to allow Groucho to give a continuous performance for an hour and a half or longer. Standard 35mm motion picture cameras were equipped with reels of film that ran 10 minutes. In normal motion picture production that was acceptable, since a 10-minute scene, filmed in one continuous take, was virtually unthinkable. On *You Bet Your Life* we didn't want to stop to reload film every 10 minutes, and we didn't want any constraints on how long we could allow the performance to run.

Our solution for continuous operation was to have two cameras in each position. While one camera was shooting, the other was being reloaded and would go back into operation again about a minute before the first camera ran out of film.

For editing, it seemed obvious that if we had one camera on Groucho, alone, all the time, and one camera on the person he was talking to, we

Four of the eight cameras used on You Bet Your Life. The top pair alternately took pictures of the two contestants or of Groucho and the contestant closest to him. The lower two cameras took turns taking close-up pictures of the contestants. The other two pairs not shown were devoted to a close-up of Groucho, every minute during the show, and a full-shot of the entire stage, including contestants, Groucho, Fenneman when he was on, and the duck when it dropped from above. Shown in the photo are the crew with our first Director of Photography James Van Trees (center in the dark suit) and to the far left, Paul Schmutz, Supervisor of the film-loading operation. In 14 years, no one ever dropped a reel of film.

should be able to cut and edit freely. For some slight variation, we had a third pair of cameras which filmed the two contestants together. Finally, we had two cameras which held a master shot, both guests and Groucho, George Fenneman when he was on stage, and the duck when it appeared from above.

The system worked. Our problem was relatively simple compared to most television programs because of the peculiarly static nature of our show. There was practically no action, except for the clash of wits and the raising of Groucho's eyebrows.

I was astonished to learn, many years later, that Groucho's first director in motion pictures, Robert Florey, had used a camera system very much like ours almost 25 years earlier. Florey, the valiant pioneer who directed the first Marx Brothers movie, *Cocoanuts,* in 1929, rolled not four, but five cameras simultaneously to capture the unpredictable brothers in action and to meet an impossible shooting schedule. While they were filming *Cocoanuts* on Long Island, the Marx Brothers were also appearing every night and in two matinees in *Animal Crackers* on Broadway. I did not learn about Florey's system from Groucho, but Hector Arce discovered it for his 1979 biography, *Groucho.*[1] Groucho's interest in the technical details of filming or staging was minimal, although he did know when his key light was out. His concern was with performance, and it was up to the rest of us to do our jobs with as little interference with the performers as possible.

We were not asking for a simple nor inexpensive process. We exposed an apparently extravagant five-and-a-half miles of 35mm black and white film each week for 11 years. On the other hand, we did not have to budget any time for rehearsal. I'm sure we would have been forced to do a live

program on television had it not been for our track record in radio, our three-year demonstration of the value of recording and editing. Broadcast live, it would not have been the same show. Several other very good comedians tried to do similar programs, all of them did the show live on television, and none of them lasted as long as *You Bet Your Life*.

You Bet Your Life's production technique was unique. Specifically designed to allow Groucho Marx to perform at his best, it worked for him and, as far as I know, has never been tried by anyone else.

TV GUIDE

How Groucho Marx Plans His Ad Libs

LOCAL PROGRAM LISTINGS
Week of March 19-25

15c

Groucho Marx

A studio publicity pose of Groucho promoting the start of his 14th season of *You Bet Your Life* **(Sept. 1960). I have no idea what he is supposed to be doing. (Courtesy Paul Wesolowski)**

The last original program of *You Bet Your Life* was broadcast on June 29, 1961. It could have gone on longer. It was still among the top 10 programs in its ratings, with 39 percent of the audience in its time period. It was calculated by the ARB rating service at that time that it was seen in 9,632,000 homes for an average audience each week of over 22 million viewers. The negotiation for its continuance chiefly concerned the time of the broadcast. We were then on at 10 o'clock in the evening, and John and Groucho felt that was too late for our viewers. It was true that our audience was somewhat tilted to the older side, but Groucho's irreverence

Candice Bergen appears with Melinda on *You Bet Your Life* **in May 1958. (Courtesy Paul Wesolowski)**

also attracted a large college-age crowd. The network was able to find an 8:30 p.m. spot on another night, but it happened to be opposite a program sponsored by one of our chief advertisers, Toni Home Hair Products. While negotiations dragged on, that time was sold to someone else, and the decision to go into re-runs was made almost by default. John Guedel says today that Groucho was willing to do another year even though he was then nearly 71 and had been a professional entertainer for 58 years. In May 1961, just before doing his last *You Bet Your Life* performance, he wrote to Norman Krasna:

> Wednesday night, the 17th of May, I wind up a fourteen-year career as the world's most prominent quiz-master. No tears will be shed by yours truly. It's done wonders for me, psychologically and financially. Physically and mentally the show has always been a romp.[2]

Candice Bergen's father, comedian and ventriloquist Edgar Bergen appeared with her on *You Bet Your Life*. Edgar did not bring his famous dummy, Charlie McCarthy, but backstage he found a willing substitute.

CHAPTER 4
John Charles Thomas and Pedro Gonzalez Gonzalez

The essence of *You Bet Your Life* was in two places: in the mind of Groucho and in the personalities of the contestants. The staff operation, then, began with finding the contestants. Unlike contemporary daytime talk shows, we did not specialize in the bizarre and sensational, and, of course, aberrant sexual behavior was automatically taboo. Our basic contestant was a normal citizen with an ordinary occupation—plumber, baker, post-office worker—a mother, a grandmother, a Girl Scout, or a set of newlyweds. But we also looked for the offbeat and unusual in the background. A couple about to be married turned out to be an Army nurse and a man who had been one of her patients. Beryl Kent was a newspaper correspondent for the *Nippon Times* who had spent three weeks as a geisha girl.

They came to us through many channels. They wrote letters, we wrote letters. Groucho was amused by a book, and we invited the author. We sent one of our scouts, Eddie Mills, to St. Louis for a week and to Long Beach, California, for another week to interview people in the showrooms of DeSoto Plymouth dealers. We read the newspapers. One of our people read that the well-known Washington hostess, Pearl Mesta, would be in town. We invited her to appear, she asked for $1,500, and we expressed our regrets. When it came to money, we ran an egalitarian show.

Public relations people of all sorts were happy to cooperate, from TWA to the Maid of Cotton Trade Group. In the late 1940s and early 1950s, the war was still much on our minds, and the Armed Services Public Relations offices were active and eager. One of our scouts read a news story about an admiral who had captured a U-boat. He called Navy Public Relations. The admiral was not available. "What other admirals do you have?" our man asked. We got the commander of the Pacific Fleet.

The well-laid plans of the public relations people didn't always work. The Naval Academy in Annapolis, Maryland was having a fund-raising drive to build a new stadium. They suggested the author C.S. Forester as a spokesman for the cause, even though his famous *Hornblower* books celebrated the British Navy. Mr. Forester agreed to appear, but seemed somewhat bemused by the whole exercise, and could not be brought to make any mention of Annapolis, in spite of three very directly leading questions by Groucho.

The great baritone, John Charles Thomas, came to us as the result of private initiative. His friend, Alfred Hay Malotte, composer of the music for the most popular setting of "The Lord's Prayer," had composed a new song, surely something entirely different, "The Golfer's Lament." Mr. Malotte wrote to us suggesting that Mr. Thomas might be willing to appear on *You Bet Your Life* if he could sing his friend's new song. We were certainly willing to accept the offer, and Mr. Thomas appeared not only to sing "The Golfer's Lament" but to return a second week to discuss rock music with his teenage partner. He was a delight on both occasions. The young lady and her mother had come to our office seeking to place the girl on the show—young Beverly Adlund was 15, cute, demure and bright, and was a good low-key partner for Mr. Thomas. She later gained considerable notoriety as the underage companion of the movie star and sometime sex symbol Errol Flynn on some well-publicized yacht trips.

Those were exceptions. *You Bet Your Life* was not a celebrity show. Less than one percent of our contestants could qualify as either famous or notorious. We did invite many special guests—an Indian chief and the president of the Elvis Presley Fan Club, a horse psychiatrist, an Italian Shakespearean actor, an organ grinder with a monkey, a baseball umpire, and, separately, a priest, a minister, and a rabbi. One special guest was a man who said he had 53 children, having been married four times. I have no recollection nor record of how the conversation went on that subject in the performance. I do, however, have a recording of the edited version, and apparently there was nothing broadcastable that Groucho could say about the situation, because the bare facts were all that was left of the interview in the broadcast.

Once a week, the "people getters," Eddie Mills, Rich Hall, and Marion Pollock, presented their catch of the week to Bernie Smith. It was a pitching process similar to the selling of a screenplay to a movie producer. The contestants were our major characters, and they brought with them our story lines. Perhaps it was a man who made his living as a

Somebody just said the secret word!

feather merchant (he actually sold feathers) or as a professional gambler, or a nurse who encountered her future spouse in a morgue, or a woman who could sing "Yes We Have No Bananas" in Polish. This, plus an attractive personality, was grist for the mill. Many of the candidates were located in response to assignments from Bernie Smith. Smith's constant concern was to put together intriguing combinations with comedy potential. The standard categories, from the beginning, had been young single people interested, as we said, "in finding the right mate," couples about to get married, newlyweds, elderly newlyweds (our scouts established a working relationship with the clerks at the marriage license bureau to identify attractive or unusual candidates), parents of young children, and mature single people whom we called bachelors and old maids. During the immediate post-war years, we had a long series of appearances of ex-GIs with their war brides from France, England, Italy, and Australia. But beyond those categories, Smith was more specific. He wanted a chiropractor and a lady wrestler, a barn dance caller and a ballet dancer, a baseball player and an umpire, and a father and mother (not related) with children under six months, the mother being under 20 and the father over 50. He read a squib in the *Reader's Digest* about a sergeant at a Coast Guard Station in Alaska whose name was Sexauer. The story was that someone had phoned the station and asked, "Do you have a Sexauer there?" and the operator replied, "Sexauer? We don't even have a coffee break!" The wheels were set in motion through Coast Guard Public Relations, Sergeant Sexauer was flown down from Alaska, appeared on *You Bet Your Life,* told the story, but very little else.

Some of our best guests had no particular qualifications at all, except vivid personalities. In September 1957, we introduced two sisters of Portuguese descent who were selected, apparently, because they both talked at the same time. They were Lena Perreira and Mercedes White.

GROUCHO:	Are you married, Lena?
MERCEDES:	Yeah, she's married.
LENA:	So is she.
GROUCHO:	Where are you from, Mercedes?
LENA:	I'm from....
MERCEDES:	We're from....
LENA:	Artesia.
MERCEDES:	We're from Artesia, California.
GROUCHO:	Where is Artesia?
LENA:	It's about....
MERCEDES:	...about four....
LENA:	...five miles....
MERCEDES:	...from Norwalk.
LENA:	It's about three miles from Norwalk, I think.
GROUCHO:	Do you live near each other?
LENA:	Well sure, three or four....
MERCEDES:	...four blocks....
LENA:	...about three to five....
MERCEDES:	...I moved.

The interview lasted four minutes. There was not one joke in the entire sequence, but the laughter was nonstop.

In the fall of 1957, we presented another pair of sisters whose qualifications seemed even less obvious. They were from Italy, one spoke English, the other didn't. Bernie somehow saw potential. Ida Tondino was the one who spoke English.

GROUCHO: How long have you been married, Ida?
IDA: 35 years.
GROUCHO: He must be a fine fellow.
IDA: *(Flatly.)* Yeah.
GROUCHO: What was there about him that made you fall in love with him?
IDA: Nothing.
GROUCHO: Well at least you didn't hate him. You must have a lot on the ball to hang on to a husband for 35 years. Are you a good cook?
IDA: Cook? Looka me!

Bernie was concerned about making them look foolish in the quiz, so he arranged for an English-speaking brother, Raymond, to be in the audience ready to come on stage and translate the questions. The first thing the brother did when he arrived on the stage was to inform Groucho that the ladies wanted to sing him a serenade. They immediately plunged into a full-voiced rendition of "O Sole Mio" which was just terrible enough to be wonderful. Halfway through, Groucho joined, his peculiar brand of harmony making theirs even worse.

After the applause, Groucho said:

> Now let's see if you can earn some money in the quiz. I doubt it, but let's see. You selected Mythology. *(He groaned.)* Raymond, you can help them. This is an unusual thing, but we're going to let him help because they've only been in this country 35 years.

IDA: Thirty-seven years.

GROUCHO:	In that case, George, you can help, too.
	(But he hadn't counted on the Italian-speaking sister, Isabella.)
GROUCHO:	What handsome youth fell in love with his own reflection in the water?
	(Raymond translates into Italian.)
ISABELLA:	Narciso.
GROUCHO:	Narcissus is right!
	Who carved a statue of a maiden and then fell in love with her?
	(Raymond translates.)
ISABELLA:	Pygmalione.
GROUCHO:	Pygmalion is right!
GEORGE:	They have two in a row right. Two more and they win a thousand dollars!
GROUCHO:	Who in mythology held up the heavens on his shoulders?
	(Translation.)
ISABELLA:	Atlante.
	(The answer on Groucho's sheet was Atlas. He looked at me. Standing off to the side, I couldn't hear clearly what she had said. It sounded a little like "Atlas," and, caught up in the spirit of the moment, I signaled to Groucho, "Right!" Checking the tape later, it was clear she had said "Atlante," and I was sure I had given her a free ride. Later, I discovered that "Atlante" is the Italian equivalent of "Atlas," and she actually was right.)
GROUCHO:	Who attached his wings with wax, flew too near the sun, and dropped into the sea?
ISABELLA:	Ichario!
GEORGE:	You have four in a row right and win a thousand dollars!
	(They decide to keep their money and not risk it on the big question. Too bad. They probably would have known that the family name of the rulers of Monaco is Grimaldi.)

Contestant Joan Fitzpatrick with Groucho in May 1959. (Courtesy Paul Wesolowski)

No matter how eccentric or unusual, our guests were always exactly what they purported to be. We hired no actors, employed no stooges, and made every effort to exclude pretenders. Our motives were more practical than ethical. If our guests tried to make up their stories, they would quickly become confused and run dry under the barrage of Groucho's questioning. The comedy in the show lay largely in a contestant's making a simple statement and Groucho's subjecting it to his panoply of comedic weapons—to reduce to absurdity, to misunderstand or misinterpret, to exaggerate, to take literally, or simply to confuse and befuddle. Our advice to the contestant was to continue to try to explain the facts or to tell the story, no matter what tangents Groucho attempted to pursue. When the guest followed our counsel, the program worked. When the guest tried to be funny, to go along with the gag, suddenly the comedy vanished.

We had a couple in their late 50s who had recently been married. The man volunteered the information that they had been married in Juvenile Court. "How did that happen?" Groucho wanted to know.

"We were juvenile delinquents," the man replied with a smirk. It was probably a little joke he had used a hundred times in telling about his marriage. This time, it bombed. There was silence. Groucho had no option but to repeat the question.

"How did you happen to be there?"

"The judge was a friend of mine," the man admitted.

"Oh, you were looking for a bargain," Groucho said. "You should have tried Thrifty Drug. They would have thrown in a bottle of shampoo."

Give Groucho a few points for effort, but it was to no avail. The audience had decided the man was a smart-aleck and didn't believe anything he said from that point on.

In at least one case I believe we were taken in by a story made of whole cloth. There existed in Hollywood at that time a small group of perhaps 10 or 15 people with no apparent occupation except to attend audience participation shows and volunteer to participate. These professional contestants or regulars did not show up in our studio very often because tickets to our show were hard to come by. One of the most familiar of these characters was Lamarr, who volunteered in every category. He once made it to the stage as a candidate for oldest bachelor, but didn't make it onto the show. But he somehow got into the studio audience every week and apparently thought he could be helpful by laughing at everything Groucho said, straight line or joke. He had a distinctive, mirthless laugh, a "har-har" that lay in the blank spaces like a wet sponge. I spent a good deal of time editing "har-hars" out of the sound tracks, until one night I went into the audience before the show and asked him please not to laugh.

The woman who, I believe, managed to pull the wool over our eyes was another professional contestant, whom I shall call Mrs. Holmes to protect the just possibly innocent. It was in October 1949, in the early years of our run, that she volunteered as a housewife with an interesting story and was sent by George Fenneman to the back of the house to talk to one of our staff. Somehow, she persuaded that person that she had a legitimate story and landed a spot on the show.

"What does your husband do, Mrs. Holmes?" Groucho asked her.

"He fills crates in a warehouse," she said.

"Fills them with what?" Groucho wanted to know.

"Anything they have to fill them with," she replied.

So far, so good.

"How did you meet him?" Groucho asked.

"I met him in a cemetery," Mrs. Holmes said.

Here we go, with the old standard cemetery story.

She proceeded to describe, with all the stock details, how she used to cut through the cemetery on her way home from work because she had a hobby of reading epitaphs. One day she stopped to read the inscription on a gravestone. It included a picture of a young man. "Gee, you're ugly," she said aloud. A voice replied, "So are you." She fainted, she said, "and when I came to, there were three gravediggers standing around me."

"Are you sure you weren't watching *Hamlet*?" Groucho asked.

Then she pulled her final coup.

"When I came to," she said, "I was sitting in a chair...."

A bell rang, a trumpet sounded, the band played "Hooray for Captain Spalding," the duck dropped down bearing a placard with the word "CHAIR," and George shouted, "She said the secret word and wins a hundred dollars!"

I had long suspected that some of our guests had accomplices in the audience signaling the secret word, and I have no proof that this was the case with Mrs. Holmes, but chair would have been an easy one to pantomime.

On rare occasions, a guest managed to top Groucho, and when it was done with grace, it was an occasion for general delight. One evening, we welcomed the Reverend James Whitcomb Brougher, past president of the American Baptist Convention and, at the time, the much-respected pastor of a large mid-town congregation. The conversation was proceeding splendidly when Groucho suddenly decided to tell him a story.

> The minister of a small southern church was having serious trouble with the amount of money in the collections. One

Groucho and a winning contestant pose for this photo. (NBC) (Courtesy Paul Wesolowski)

Sunday morning he addressed the congregation from the pulpit. "Brothers and sisters," he said, "I have to tell you that the collections have been mighty small lately, mighty small. So I have decided to leave this pulpit—

—here Groucho left his lectern and strode across the stage—

and as I pass among you, you will notice the piece of mistletoe I have pinned to the tail of my coat."

Groucho returned to his lectern with an expression of delighted satisfaction at the audience response, calling out to me as he passed, "I know we can't use it, but I had to do it." Settling down on his stool, he said to the minister, "You can use that, Doc, if you want to."

Dr. Brougher smiled and said:

> You remind me of what Will Rogers once
> said about a fellow, "His mind is like a race
> horse. Runs better on a dirt track."

On another program, our guests were an elderly couple, married over 50 years. Groucho asked the woman to remember what the man had said when he proposed to her.

MABLE: Well, I guess he told me I had a nice big trunk, and I....

GROUCHO: You had a big trunk?

MABLE: Well, we were on the road in Vaudeville, you see, and he had a small trunk for his props and costumes, but I had quite a large trunk, and I guess he thought there would be plenty of room for both our clothes, so we could travel together.
(That legitimate explanation gave Groucho the basis for a running gag throughout the rest of the interview. A little later, he was speaking to Mable.)

GROUCHO: What would you do if you found him chasing a beautiful young blonde? Make him give the trunk back?

MABLE: I don't think he could do much chasing, not at his age.

GROUCHO: Mable, you have no idea how innocent you are!
Ed, what did you do in the evening when you were courting?

ED: Oh, we'd go out buggy riding.

GROUCHO: Take the trunk with you? Did you just keep driving?

ED: *(With a delightful, dry, hesitant delivery.)* Well, yes, we'd drive until we found a nice shady spot under a tree, and we'd stop and let the horse cool off.

GROUCHO: Are you sure it was the horse that needed cooling off?

In a few cases, guests came to us with a little package of prepared material, and we just let them go. Judge Leroy Dawson of the Los Angeles Municipal Court was one of the most successful. Judge Dawson had earned a national reputation during his tenure on traffic court, and he had a polished routine that he had doubtless used at numerous Rotary and Kiwanis Club luncheons.

"Last year, I had 2,500 customers, and not one of them was satisfied," was his opening. The Judge had a wonderfully sly, precise diction, a parody on the pedantic.

"The average Los Angeles driver drives as though he had just bought the street. He drives as though his license was a title and not a right to use."

Groucho, recognizing another pro, let him go, mostly without interruption.

"When they come to court, I say, 'You're charged with driving in excess of the speed limit,' and they say, 'Guilty, your honor, BUT!' Now I'm going to get a five-minute speech on why this guy is so important socially, politically, and economically...."

GROUCHO: He means he can break you.
JUDGE: That's what *he* thinks. No, he just wants to explain why he shouldn't be required to pay the prevailing scale.
GROUCHO: He's got a point, if it's me.

John Robert Sweeney and his wife, Helen, from Glasgow, Scotland, were a delightful young couple who also brought some material with them. Earlier in the interview, however, a charming passage occurred when Groucho asked Helen, "What is a courtship like in Scotland? Where did Johnny take you for excitement?"

She thought for a moment and then said, "The war was on at the time, so there wasn't very much we could do. There was a blackout."

The audience was ahead of Groucho on this one, and the laughter was already growing when he spoke, in a philosophical tone, "No, I guess there's not much a young couple can do in a blackout."

GROUCHO: Do you know any good Scottish jokes, Helen?
HELEN: No, I haven't got much of a sense of humor.
GROUCHO: Neither have I, but I still like to tell Scottish jokes. Did you hear the one about the Scotsman who had

Mrs. Housing Development, a contestant, poses with Groucho during the 1960-61 season (the final year) of *You Bet Your Life*. This was an elaborate promotion invented by John Guedel. I never did understand it. (Courtesy Paul Wesolowski)

	himself tattooed so he wouldn't have to buy his family a television set? How do you like that?
HELEN:	*(Grudgingly)* It's funny.
GROUCHO:	You think it's funny, eh? Well, I agree. You certainly don't have a very good sense of humor. What about you, John, do you know any good Scottish jokes?
JOHN:	Yes, I know a few. Have you heard the one about the Scotsman who was traveling on the train down to England, and the conductor came along for his fare. He said, "That'll be five shillings." The Scotsman

says, "I'll give you three and six." The conductor says, "Five shillings is the price." The Scotsman says, "It's no worth any more than three and six. I'll give you three and six." The conductor he lost his temper at this. He seized the Scotsman's suitcase and hurled it out the window. At this, the Scotsman burst into tears. He said, "First of all, you try to do me out of one and six, and then to crown it all, you throw me own son out the window."

We had an Australian joke one evening, too. A woman guest told about the American soldier who woke up in an Australian hospital. "Oh nurse," he said, "did they bring me here to die?" And she said, "No, they brought you here yesterdie."

I also particularly liked the little girl who wasn't intending to make a joke, but replied to Groucho's stock question, "What do you want to be when you grow up?" by pausing for a moment and then saying, "A woman."

Probably our best-remembered contestant was Pedro Gonzalez Gonzalez, a young Mexican-American boy who had grown up on the Texas-Mexican border. His family had had an itinerant Vaudeville act in which he sang and danced and played odd musical instruments. In 1952, he was working in a television station in San Antonio, Texas, as a general handy man, pulling cables for the cameras and doing odd jobs. Walter O'Keefe came to town to do a telethon for cerebral palsy. In the late hours of the night they ran out of acts, and Pedro persuaded O'Keefe to let him go on. He sang and danced and played the skillet with a spoon and danced with Dagmar, the statuesque blonde. He was a big hit with the sparse late-night audience in San Antonio. Back in Hollywood, one of O'Keefe's staff told our man, Eddie Mills, who tracked Pedro down at the San Antonio TV station and sent him $300 for a plane ticket to Los Angeles. Pedro put $200 in the bank and bought a bus ticket. As soon as Bernie Smith talked to him, he knew he had a prize and booked him for the performance of January 7, 1953. Except for the telethon, it would be the first show Pedro had ever done in English.

It is especially hard to capture the flavor of that interview because much of it depended on the cadence of Pedro's speech, and on some magic chemistry that was immediately created between him and Groucho.

Groucho poses with Pedro Gonzalez Gonzalez.

GROUCHO: Your name is Ramiro Gonzalez Gonzalez. Why do you have Gonzalez twice?

PEDRO: I'm Ramiro Gonzalez Gonzalez because my father before he married my mother she was Gonzalez.

GROUCHO: Would you give me that again?

PEDRO: My father was Gonzalez before he married my mother. My mother was Gonzalez before she married my father.

GROUCHO: What does your wife call you? Ramiro or Gonzalez?

PEDRO: She call me Pedro.

He sang and he danced, but mostly he talked in fractured English, and the audience loved it.

GROUCHO: Pedro, we could do a great act together. We could make a tour of Vaudeville, you and I. What should we call our act? Two Hot Tamales?

PEDRO:	No, we would call it Gonzalez, Gonzalez & Marx.
GROUCHO:	That's great. Two people in the act and I get third billing.

So, okay, we gave Pedro his feed line. It worked, and the exchange was perfectly in character for both of them.

Pedro left the studio and caught the next bus back to San Antonio.

Six weeks later, the show hit the air and a star was born. The William Morris Agency sent a man in a blue suit to San Antonio.

"I live in the Mexican section, you know. They never seen an American there," Pedro said. "I thought it was a bill collector."

The William Morris man had a contract for him to make a movie with John Wayne, starting in two weeks.

"I can't make no movies," Pedro said. "I don't read and write."[1]

He learned. The contract with John Wayne lasted for almost 20 years. He became a star attraction at rodeos and county fairs, and, finally, he did so much good work in the Mexican-American community that San Antonio named a municipal park after him.

After Bernie Smith made his selection of contestants, the potential guests were assigned to one of our writers. Usually there were only two writers plus Bernie. Hy Freedman was senior man, who was with us through the entire run of the show. He had previously written comedy material for Steve Allen, *Duffy's Tavern* and Red Skelton. Elroy Schwartz was with us for a year, as was Ed "Doc" Tyler, an interesting case in that he was a world-renowned authority on infertility, with an active medical practice. He just liked to write puns. Finally, Howard Harris joined our staff, and he and Hy were the team for the remaining 12 years.

Howard had written for a number of comedy shows, notably *The Honeymooners*, *The Tonight Show,* and *The Jimmy Durante Show* and had been one of the uncredited writers on the Marx Brothers' film *A Night in Casablanca* and Groucho's movie *Copacabana.*

The procedure was for the writers to conduct extensive interviews with the candidates, usually two to three hours, and then write a complete script.

The scripts from the writers went to Bernie Smith who did a re-write and passed it along to John Guedel for his perusal and contributions. Finally, we took it to Groucho.

Every Tuesday morning for 14 years, Bernie Smith and I made the trek up the hill to Groucho's Beverly Hills home bearing the script for the following week's performance. He went through it line by line, changing words and phrases, adding jokes, throwing some out.

The conclusion from all this would seem to be that the entire show was scripted. Not so. Going into performance, we did have a full script with jokes and routines and many open questions. During that performance, both Groucho and the guests made their contributions. Some of those additions were retained in the final broadcast. Some were rejected. Some of the original script was retained in the final broadcast. Some was rejected. An analysis of a typical program is illuminating. On the program broadcast on November 15, 1950, we presented three couples: a construction worker and a housewife, a Swiss war bride and her American husband, and a home economics teacher and a typical husband.

Pedro turned his *You Bet Your Life* appearance into a film career with John Wayne.

	Written Jokes	Broadcast Jokes	Groucho Ad Libs	Broadcast Ad Libs
1st Interview	19	7	7	5
2nd Interview	16	2	5	5
3rd Interview	18	6	5	4
Total	53	15	17	14

In addition, there were in the script 30 open questions with no responses indicated for either Groucho or the guests. Of these, 19 proved to be productive and were included, with the resulting conversation, in the broadcast.

The fact that not all of Groucho's improvised lines were included in the broadcast was significant. Because of the protection of the editing process, he knew he could take chances, say the first thing that came to his mind, without having to employ his own censor, allowing him to be at his uninhibited creative best.

It was a unique theatrical form that Groucho became the master of on *You Bet Your Life*. He had long practiced the art of inserting improvised lines into a structured script, or of ringing variations on his own speeches in a prepared dialogue. But in *You Bet Your Life* he faced a situation in which he could not be absolutely certain what the other person would say. The lines in a dialogue were frequently written for the contestants, but there was no guarantee that they would be delivered as planned. Groucho had to be ready, therefore, to shift verbal gears at any moment to suit the demands of the lines that were fed to him. And it was this challenge that was one of his chief pleasures in doing *You Bet Your Life*.

The complex system of contestant cueing was, I believe, invented by John Guedel and certainly perfected by him on his programs *People Are Funny* and *House Party*. In those enterprises, he had the collaboration of another master of improvisation, Art Linkletter. The system also required the training of writers, primarily in the preparation of scripts that recognized how far one could go in feeding lines to amateurs and still maintain credibility. Sometimes, especially on *People Are Funny* and *House Party*, the information had to be very simple so that it could be conveyed quickly, perhaps on the way from the studio audience to the stage:

> When he asks you if your husband's snor-
> ing bothers you, you say "Yes."

Sometimes that was all that was necessary to set up a routine. Most often, however, there was time to take the victim backstage for a few minutes with the writer in a cueing room. Then the speeches that were suggested could be slightly more complicated, but not too much so. It was also important that the information be true and honest, since it would have been extremely awkward should a contestant have changed his mind onstage.

Pre-show with contestants and Groucho's stand-in, who was a barber. They helped the cameraman check his lighting and also allowed Groucho to show up just before the show. This photo also shows the new set after we finally got rid of the drapes and two new sponsors who came on board when DeSoto dropped out during the last few years of the show. The set doesn't look much like the *Millionaire* set—no flashing lights or electronic scoreboard; but it worked.

On *You Bet Your Life,* of course, the preparation for contestant participation in most cases began well in advance of the performance. By the time they reached the studio, the information about most contestants had been culled from lengthy preliminary interviews, distilled into script form, rewritten, and refined by Bernie Smith and John Guedel, and finally reviewed by Groucho and me. Then, on the evening of the performance, the guests met with their partners, whom they had usually never seen before, in a session lasting about a half hour in one of the little cueing rooms. There they had a chance to reconsider any statements they had made in their preliminary interviews and to make any corrections of fact that might be necessary. Chiefly, however, these sessions were designed to give them time to absorb the new wording that had frequently been imposed on their statements, designed to preserve the truth of the concept but still give Groucho a chance to make a play on words, pretend a temporary misunderstanding, or pursue a hopefully comic tangent. Miraculously, it almost always worked. If it didn't, I cut it out.

A good example of cueing occurred on the broadcast of January 16, 1952. Our scouts had located Mrs. Lucille Goldner, who was a chinchilla rancher. (This was in the days when it was still OK to talk about raising animals for fur.) She had been thoroughly interviewed in advance, the information gleaned had been organized into a script and reviewed with her on the night of the performance. Although it was fairly lengthy and somewhat detailed, there was no problem in her remembering the facts because they had all come from her in the first place. The only trick was to persuade her to reveal the information a little bit at a time and in the sequence we suggested, simply by answering the specific questions. The dialogue went as follows:

GROUCHO: What is a chinchilla?

MRS. GOLDNER: It's a very beautiful small rodent with very dense fur. It has up to 100 hairs out of each follicle. You only have one.

GROUCHO: Let's keep this on an impersonal basis. I don't mind your describing a rat, but don't include me in it. Why would someone want to waste his time on rodents when there are so many other ways of wasting your time?

MRS. GOLDNER: Maybe because a full-length chinchilla coat costs approximately $7,500.

GROUCHO: Well, how many of these coats can you make from a chinchilla?

MRS. GOLDNER: It takes approximately 200 chinchillas to make one coat.

GROUCHO: Sounds like they have a powerful union, these lads. How much would a good chinchilla cost me?

MRS. GOLDNER: I'll sell you a nice chinchilla for $500.

GROUCHO: Wait a minute. One chinchilla isn't going to do me any good. I wasn't born yesterday, you know. How much would a pair cost?

MRS. GOLDNER: A good breeding pair would cost about $1,650.

GROUCHO: Apparently these chinchillas weren't born yes-
                         terday, either.

Essentially all she had to remember was to give the price of a single chinchilla first and wait for Groucho to ask for the price of a pair. It's also important to note that Groucho needed the script here, too. We could certainly not expect him to improvise those questions in that order on the spur of the moment.

We had a different case on the broadcast of September 16, 1953. In that instance, it was not so important for the contestant to repeat exactly what she said, but, more important, to reproduce the manner in which she said it. Mrs. Marian Shaw was apparently chosen because of her incoherence. In telling how she met her husband, she spoke in broken phrases, with scarcely a recognizable complete sentence in the whole discourse. That quality was identified in her preliminary interview, and the script was organized to capitalize on it.

GROUCHO: What did he say when he proposed?
MRS. SHAW: Oh, something... he mumbled something... I don't
               know... I couldn't tell... but I said yes.
GROUCHO: He might have been asking if your shoes hurt.

We never said directly that Groucho did not have a script. We simply never said that he did, and we never identified anyone on our staff as a writer. Their names did appear on the screen in the later years, however. The writers, along with the people getters, were listed as program staff. Bernie Smith shared my credit as director, and, finally, he and I were listed as producers with John Guedel as executive producer. We made no claim that the guests walked off the street directly up to the microphone. We simply never admitted that anyone had ever talked to them in advance. We did say that Groucho never talked to them before he met them onstage. That was true. We never said that Groucho did not have a cueing device that allowed him to read the script on camera. But we did go to considerable lengths to conceal that fact from the audience and the public.

Our secret weapon was an instrument whose trade name was "the Visualizer." It was an overhead projector of the type familiar in classrooms. I thought of applying it to our purposes when I saw it used to keep score in a bowling alley. For our use, we built a large box with a rear-projection screen and placed it just to the left of Groucho's close-up camera. It was almost in his direct line of sight to the contestants, so that when he was looking at it, he seemed to be looking at one of the guests.

The entire script was transferred by hand, using a grease pencil, to transparent plastic sheets. A young man named Chuck Wohler was inside the enclosure behind the screen in communication by intercom with Bernie Smith, offstage. There was a good deal of shuffling of pages during the performance as Groucho adapted the script to the needs of the moment, re-wording lines, skipping speeches, inserting alternative versions. Many times when a guest was proving to be unproductive, we decided in mid-interview to abandon the pre-conceived context and turn to the other guest, or simply jump to the quiz. There was always a point in every script marked "Skip to here."

Even though Groucho appeared relaxed on the screen, the whole process took enormous concentration on his part, and it was a primary part of my job to be sure that nothing distracted his attention. The entire physical set-up of lights and cameras and personnel was calculated to eliminate all possible distraction. The complicated process of reloading four cameras every 10 minutes almost in front of his eyes was carried out with the utmost care, like a ballet. Under the supervision of Paul Schmutz of Filmcraft, I don't believe anyone ever dropped a can of film.

The one time that I violated the rule against unnecessary distraction was the one time I can ever remember Groucho's speaking harshly to me. During the performance, I was always close at hand, just out of camera range, usually crouched down to be as unobtrusive as possible, ready in case he needed me to solve some misunderstanding or mix-up in logistics. I rarely intervened in the interviews, except when Groucho requested it, but there were occasionally times during the quiz when he was uncertain whether an answer was correct and would turn to me for clarification.

On the evening in question, in 1956, we were using a quiz in which the contestants had to answer four questions in a row correctly to win $1,000. Two wrong answers in a row and they were out. We had a couple who answered three questions in a row correctly, then missed one, and repeated the cycle several times. Consequently, we had almost run through the list of 20 prepared questions in the category they had selected.

George said, "You now have three right, again. One more right and you win the $1,000."

Groucho said, "I have only two questions left in this category. If you get one of them right, I'll give you the $1,000 anyway."

It was a rule Groucho made up on the spur of the moment. I said something from my crouched position in an attempt to clarify the situation. It's inaudible on the recording, but whatever it was, it was enough to destroy Groucho's concentration, and he turned to me and said, "You keep out of this!" The audience laughed. Groucho said to them, "A strange gnome is whining in back of me here. It finally gets on your nerves." The couple proceeded to miss the next question, but answered the last one on the list and won the $1,000.

Nothing further was said that evening, but several days later I received a letter on Groucho's stationery.

> Dear Bob:
> Here it is. Sorry I snapped at you on the
> set, but you can be provoking.
> Best,
> Groucho

You Bet Your Life was filmed for television every Wednesday evening in the NBC studios at Sunset and Vine. These were converted radio studios, used before NBC built its plant in Burbank. The studio was designed for us, an intimate house of about 500, with the seating raised to look over the cameras to the stage. One firm specification was that Groucho must have eye contact with at least one section of the audience, and, since our staging was so static and unchanging, we could specify exactly where that location should be. Groucho was always seated stage right facing across stage, so we extended the left side of the house to be directly in his line of sight. It was one of the weekly tasks of Eddie Mills to inspect the line waiting outside the studio and select a pretty, preferably blonde, preferably buxom young woman whom he would escort to a seat in the front row. This exercise was designed to allow Groucho to say each week during the pre-show warm-up:

> There's a pretty girl in the front row with
> a loose sweater. I'd prefer a loose girl with
> a tight sweater. How I'd love to pull the
> wool over her eyes.

The audience was, in fact, the third active element, besides Groucho and the contestants, in the production of *You Bet Your Life.* In every Groucho performance since the mule-engendered audience response in Nacogdoches, the audience had always been a participant. As long as they were laughing, the performer had a set of guideposts to follow. Without the laughter, he was clueless.

In a Groucho performance, there was no fourth wall. Even in the movies, he broke the barrier to speak directly to the audience. During the studio sessions of *You Bet Your Life,* I always kept the house lights at half power so he could see the audience. Even in the theatrical production of Groucho's play *Time For Elizabeth* when we toured the summer theatres, I kept the house lights at a quarter full so he could see the faces.

During most of the run of *You Bet Your Life* on both radio and television, our audio engineer was Art Brearley. I had worked with him on many other programs, including *People Are Funny* and *The Red Skelton Show*, and I knew he was the best in the business at maintaining a perfect balance between the dialogue on the stage and the reactions of the studio audience. It is not a simple thing, audience response. It can range from a sudden silence, a sharp collective intake of breath, through an almost inaudible expression of unease, to a roar of disapproval. There can be giggles and chuckles and single guffaws or that wonderful explosion when 500 people are surprised by joy. There are few satisfactions comparable to that which results when a performer delivers a line and a crowded house explodes in a full-bodied laugh expressing surprise, delight and approval. That may be topped by the phenomenon I observed time and again when Groucho and our troupe were touring the New England summer theatres in *Time For Elizabeth*. It came at the moment when Groucho walked onstage and the entire audience rose and seemed to say, "We love you." They were clearly paying tribute to an entire career, offering thanks for a lifetime of pleasure. It was close to being a group embrace, almost palpable from the stage.

Audience reaction was my guide in editing, also. The general rule was, no laugh, no joke. But the audience wasn't infallible. Sometimes the laughter was engendered by something other than enjoyment. Occasionally, it was embarrassment, sometimes shock, as it usually is in response to four-letter words or, in some venues, simply because it is the expected response, an evidence of being "in."

Often our audience had a mind of its own, interpreting a remark in ways never intended or seeing a dirty meaning in an innocent line,

On the radio show when our sponsor was Elgin-American, each contestant was given one of the sponsor's compacts or cigarette cases. The constants were encouraged to be suitably appreciative. (Courtesy Paul Wesolowski)

surprising even Groucho. One evening, our guest was a very personable and proper young man from Pakistan. In some mysterious way, the conversation got around to the subject of vegetables. "Do you get them fresh," Groucho wanted to know, "or are they canned?"

"There are no cans in Pakistan," the young man said firmly.

There was no pause for consideration between the line and the laughter. The audience jumped immediately to the earthy interpretation. Groucho, following his dictum of "no terlet jokes," said nothing. The censor didn't like the whole thing, and, following 1950 standards, that piece of film landed on the cutting room floor.

Some laughter in our studio was because the audience felt it was expected of them. George Fenneman and Groucho had just spent a half hour encouraging the group to loosen their inhibitions and making it clear to them that theirs was an important function. And some laughter was simply because of the assumption that whatever Groucho said was ipso facto funny.

All of the laughter heard on the *You Bet Your Life* broadcasts was the actual laughter of that particular audience to that specific joke. We never, ever, inserted a laugh because we thought a line was funny. I often deleted a joke simply because it got no laugh. Five hundred of our peers had passed judgment.

Groucho himself rarely laughed during a performance, but when he did it was a beautiful sight to see. Perhaps once or twice in a season something a guest said would strike him as so ludicrous he could not resist a full-blown, head-back, hearty laugh. He also told me of those rare occasions when all five Marx Brothers would meet for dinner and finally, inevitably, some remark, usually, he said, by Zeppo, would set them off into an uncontrollable falling-off-chairs fit of laughter.

In contrast, I am reminded of some of the times I joined him for lunch at Hillcrest Country Club to sit with him at the Comedians' Round Table, where the guests included Harpo (Chico was more likely to be at The Friars in Hollywood), George Burns, Jack Benny, George Jessel, Phil Silvers, some writers, including Irving Brecher, creator of *The Life of Riley*, and, usually, someone's dentist, agent, or lawyer. The participants saved their best material for the occasion, the jokes were constant and, usually, of a high order. Jack Benny mostly listened and never laughed. When he heard a joke he approved of, he simply slapped his hand three times on the table. The rest of the participants were satisfied with the accolade.

I recall another occasion that says something about the peculiar nature of laughter, underlining the fact that it is, generally, a social phenomenon. Groucho and I were in his combination office and bedroom. We were on our way to some kind of a function and, as we reached the door, we were both stopped by the picture on the screen of the television set. It was the stateroom scene from *A Night at the Opera,* certifiably one of the funniest scenes ever filmed, capable of producing gales of laughter in a theatre. Groucho and I stood there watching, silently, not laughing, not even smiling. When it was over, he switched the set off.

"Funny scene," I said.

"Yes," he said.

Getting the contestants to the stage and onto the program was not a simple matter. At first, John Guedel thought that it was important to be able to say that the guests were "selected by our studio audience just before we went on the air." In the beginning, that was literally true. We invited two people for each category—two legal secretaries, two lumberjacks, even, one time, two nuclear physicists, two pairs of newlyweds—and the final selection for each category was, indeed, made by the studio audience.

George Fenneman was in charge of the pre-program activities. He would summon these invited guests to the stage—the two plumbers, cowboys, bachelors, or new parents—and put them through a series of simple contests. "You are a door-to-door salesman. I'm a housewife. Sell me one of your new line of girdles." Or, "...sell me a cow." Other tests were even simpler. "Name all the movies (or animals, or vegetables) beginning with the letter 'C' that you can think of in 30 seconds." Sometimes he used a ludicrous physical stunt which was more entertaining to the audience than valid as a test. It was the "orange game" which had been developed on *People Are Funny*. Each pair of contestants was given an orange. One of them tucked it under his chin, and the trick was to pass it to his partner without either of them using their hands. This was used mostly when choosing pairs of newlyweds or engaged couples. After all the tests, George would hold his hand over each contestant's head, and the audience would indicate by its applause which one they wanted for the program. It was, of course, more a test of personality

The famous stateroom scene in *A Night at the Opera* (MGM, 1935).

than of skill, but simplistic as it was, it usually resulted in the choice of an attractive guest.

The audience selection process did have serious drawbacks, however, in the preparation of the script. Both of the potential contestants had been interviewed in advance, but since the writer could not know which one would be chosen, the questions and the jokes had to be generic, with no specific personal references. We could ask questions and make jokes about plumbers in general, but not about this particular plumber, his idiosyncrasies and personal experiences, since we did not know which of the two would be chosen. Fairly soon, the advantage of dealing with more specific material became apparent, and George began to introduce special guests—a specific prize-fighter, a man who raised worms for sale, a Congressional medal-of-honor winner. The method of selecting contestants also changed. When our scouts had found a potentially good guest, let's say an elderly man with grandchildren and some good stories, and he had been interviewed and a script had been written, he was then invited to the show and placed in the auditorium before the other members of the audience arrived. Then George could say, "We're looking for grandfathers this evening." Volunteers were sent to the back of the house to talk to members of our staff, and our pre-selected, planted grandfather would be chosen. This would allow George to say on the air with some degree of credibility as far as the studio audience was concerned, "Just before we went on the air, we selected a grandfather from our studio audience." We persuaded ourselves that this amount of deceit was in a good cause.

Eventually, however, even that device was abandoned. During most of the show's run, at least one contestant on every program was actually selected by the audience, but special guests—and equally specially prepared scripts—began to predominate. "We asked for some people with interesting backgrounds...." It turned out that she owned a baseball team and he lived in a tree. "Before we went on the air [literally true, but a long time before], we selected a married couple, Mr. & Mrs. Everett Calecoate." They had a family of eight children, who were invited up from the audience to sing and did so beautifully.

Occasionally, George himself was credited with the discovery. "I saw an interesting article in the newspaper about a married couple and told them to come to see us the next time they were in Hollywood." They had been walking all over the country, from border to border, in order

Two contestants from the radio show in a posed photo after the show. Groucho was not interested in the man with the bag of money! (Courtesy Paul Wesolowski)

to lose weight. Someone had seen the article, although it wasn't literally George.

There was a huge advantage for our writers in having the contestants to work with. Unlike most comedy shows, we did not have to start from scratch each week to create a new batch of jokes about pedestrians, smog, women drivers, the high cost of living, and politics—the stock in trade of every comedian in the business. Our contestants brought the raw material to us, and our staff became highly expert at converting it into the stuff of laughter.

As a contender in the perennial truth-versus-fiction contest, I submit the following, which occurred on April 9, 1952.

GROUCHO: How long have you been married, Herman?
HERMAN: Five years the first time, 30 years the second time.
GROUCHO: What happened to the first marriage?
HERMAN: My mother-in-law came to visit.

GROUCHO: Say no more, Herman, I understand perfectly. How
                did you meet number two?
HERMAN: I married my mother-in-law.

There you have six months of a soap-opera plot in six lines.

On *You Bet Your Life,* by the time the contestants reached our stage, we had a pretty good idea of what they had to say, but we could never be sure of exactly how they were going to say it, or even absolutely sure that they would remember to say it at all.

There were, however, many structured sequences which proceeded exactly as written, with the guests giving the precise responses expected. On our first television show, broadcast October 5, 1950, George introduced a young couple about to be married. The following dialogue ensued:

GROUCHO: What sort of work do you do, Joe?
JOE: I work for Owens Illinois Glass Company.
GROUCHO: Where is Owens, Illinois?
JOE: In Vernon, California.
GROUCHO: Owens, Illinois is in Vernon, California? Does Rand
                McNally know about this?
JOE: Owens Illinois has a plant in Vernon, California.
GROUCHO: And where is Owens, Illinois?
JOE: There is no such place as Owens, Illinois.
GROUCHO: You just said it was in Vernon, California! Mary,
                where do you work?
MARY: I work at Owens Illinois, too.
GROUCHO: For a town that doesn't exist, Owens, Illinois has a
                bigger population than Vernon, California. This kind
                of publicity could put Owens on the map, after all.

The obvious reason the whole thing worked is that Joe and Mary merely had to tell the truth. There were times when we simply gave the guest a line to say. If it was in character, it sometimes worked. If it didn't, I cut it out. In 1948, with a young couple about to be married, Groucho offered the pretty young woman a dollar to let him kiss her. She refused. He raised the offer to two dollars. No sale.

GROUCHO: Last chance. Five dollars.
MAN: Take the five dollars. It can't be that bad.

Groucho welcomes newlyweds Carol and Carl Halverstadt.

The writers pushed the formula pretty close to its limit for our show in May 1950 in an interview with identical twin sisters, Janey and Joey Pope. The routine worked because the young women were very bright and understood entirely the game we were playing.

GROUCHO: Janey, where are you from?

JANEY: Los Angeles.

GROUCHO: Joey, where were you born — Walla Walla?

JOEY: No, I was born in St. Louis.
(She might naturally have said, "We were born...." but she understood the set-up, and this answer was credible.)

GROUCHO: You're identical twins, your sister was born in Los Angeles, and you were born in St. Louis! Just as I thought! You're twin fakes!
You'd better explain.

JOEY: We were born in St. Louis, but we call Los Angeles our home.

GROUCHO: Janey, how can your teachers tell you apart?

JANEY: They can tell us apart when we're together, but when we're not together, it's pretty hard to tell us apart.

(This may seem too complicated to expect her to re-
member, but these were her own words which she had
probably said hundreds of times before, and besides,
they were true.)

GROUCHO: Joey, would you mind going over what she just said? Slowly and succinctly.

JOEY: What she means is, when we're separated, it's harder to tell us apart than it is when we're together, because when we're together you can tell us apart.

GROUCHO: *(To the other twin.)* Would you mind telling me what she means?

JANEY: What we mean is that when we're together you can see some differences.

GROUCHO: *(To the same girl, but calling her by the wrong name.)* Joey, does everybody have the same trouble?

JANEY: I'm Janey.

GROUCHO: I don't care about that anymore. Answer my question. Does everybody have my trouble?

JANEY: I don't know. What's your trouble?

Sometimes the system hit a snag, however. Occasionally, a contestant had second thoughts, and the dialogue did not flow exactly as anticipated.

In the years after the Second World War, some of our most successful interviews were with young women from foreign countries who had married American servicemen. Early in 1949, our guests were a young woman from Italy and her ex-G.I. husband. Groucho asked her, "How did you meet Stewart, Adriana?"

What followed was entirely up to her. She was simply told in advance that she would be asked that question and was encouraged to tell it the way it happened.

ADRIANA: My sister was sick with pneumonia. They needed penicillin, and we didn't have any. I was so desperate I just ran out in the street and stopped the first American I met. It was him. He helped me.

GROUCHO: *(Ad lib.)* Stewart, do you always carry penicillin around with you?

STEWART:	No. I had to search. I had to look quite a while.
GROUCHO:	*(Script.)* When you were courting Adriana, what love tokens did you lay at her feet?

In the script it was suggested that he mention "stuff swiped from the Army mess hall—Spam, bread, beans, Vienna sausage, powdered eggs and milk." He probably told our interviewer about these things, or perhaps his wife did, but when it came time to face the nation on our show, he was unwilling to repeat it. Bernie Smith may have been influenced by what he knew was going on among some G.I.'s in Italy during the war when he was an aide to General Mark Clark. He would not have put it in the script, however, if neither the man nor his wife had said it.

What Stewart finally said, after a bit of encouragement by Groucho, was, "Well, there were very few things you could find along that line— flour..." (and after some hesitation) "...canned soup."

The script called for Groucho to say, "You had your own Marshall plan." He decided that what the man had said was not enough to support that. Instead, he invented his own line, using what the woman had told him earlier.

"Flour, canned soup, and penicillin! What more could a girl want?"

The audience was delighted, Stewart's honor was preserved, and the story was neatly rounded off.

In November 1950, our first couple was introduced as "an Irish war bride and her husband." Groucho greeted the young woman with some scripted dialect.

GROUCHO:	Faith and begorra and Barry Fitzgerald. Sure it's a foine thing to be afther havin' ye here with us this night, sure as me name's Grouch O'Marx! Now, does that make you feel at home?
WOMAN:	No, they don't talk like that where I come from.
GROUCHO:	Well, where do they talk like that!
WOMAN:	I don't think they talk like that anywhere.

One of Groucho's most quoted lines was included in the profile when he appeared on *Time* magazine's cover on December 31, 1951. *Time* said:

Groucho's jokes sound far funnier than they read afterward. But there are exceptions, such as the one when he asked a tree surgeon, "Tell me, Doc, did you ever fall out of a patient?"

Time then contrasted this to another remark when a shapely young school teacher told him that geometry was the study of lines, curves, and surfaces. "Kiss me, you fool!" Groucho said. [2] As *Time* noted, the tree surgeon line reads better than the geometry line. But "Kiss me, you fool!" got a yell from the audience, and "fall out of a patient" a mild chuckle. Furthermore, "fall out of a patient" was not an improvised line. I suspect that Bernie Smith thought of the line first and then sent our scouts out to look for a likely tree surgeon.

There are 19 other tree jokes in that script for March 31, 1949 which aired April 13. They range from the obvious, "Do you have a branch office?" which the audience did not find amusing, to a fanciful remark about a tree psychiatrist who treats nut trees. They laughed at that one. Of the 19 written tree jokes, seven survived the editing process.

There were other cases in which the contrived and the improvised were so entangled as to be virtually inextricable. One evening in October 1957, George introduced a guest as "a Los Angeles cab driver who says he is a perennial dissenter. He wants to discuss one of the answers he gave in the quiz several weeks ago. Henry Piffle *(pronounced approximately, Piffleh)*, meet Groucho Marx."

After a brief discussion of the proper pronunciation of his name, Mr. Piffle said, "I came here to protest. You remember a few weeks ago I was on your show, you asked me a question...."

GROUCHO: I ask everybody questions, Henry.

MR. PIFFLE: Yeah, but this particular question, the first question on the quiz, was, "What is a pachyderm?" I said it was a prehistoric animal, and you said, "Better luck next time." So I went home and picked up Webster's Dictionary. *(Reading from a piece of paper.)* "Pachyderm—member of the pachydermata group of thick-skinned animals, especially the elephant and the rhinoceros." A little further down, it says, "Mastodon." An elephant is a pachyderm. The mastodon is an

Groucho is named Outstanding Television personality of 1950 by the Academy of Television Arts and Sciences. Presenting the award is Miss America Rosemary LaPlanche. (Courtesy Paul Wesolowski)

ancestor of the elephant. A mastodon is a pre-historic animal, therefore....

GROUCHO: All right, let's stop right there. You realize that I am just the quizmaster up here, and I read things off a piece of paper. I have no more knowledge than you have, perhaps less, about most subjects. Mr. Bob Dwan, the director of our show, was a student who graduated with high honors from Stanford University [*correct, except for the "high honors"*]. I will bring him out here, and you discuss it with Mr. Dwan and

"Senator" Dudley LeBlanc, housewife Audrey Cooper, and Groucho February 1951. (Courtesy Paul Wesolowski)

	leave me out of it. Bob, will you come out here a minute? *(Dwan enters, shakes hands with Piffle.)* You've met Mr. Piffle.
MR. PIFFLE:	Piffleh.
GROUCHO:	I don't care what it is, I'm leaving.
DWAN:	I'm not staying very long. I understand that your point is that some prehistoric animals were pachyderms.
MR. PIFFLE:	Yes.

DWAN:	And you say that elephants are pachyderms.
MR. PIFFLE:	Yes.
DWAN:	And that therefore we should have considered this a correct answer.
MR. PIFFLE:	Definitely.
DWAN:	If I can recall my college logic, this is an incorrect syllogism that you are attempting to apply here.
MR. PIFFLE:	That's worse than pachyderm!
DWAN:	There is a classic example of this. You say, "All cats are animals, all dogs are animals, therefore, all dogs are cats." This is an incorrect syllogism with an undistributed middle, and I'm afraid we must still consider that "prehistoric animal" was an incorrect answer to, "What is a pachyderm?"
MR. PIFFLE:	It's a bum deal.
	(Groucho shakes hands with Dwan.)
MR. PIFFLE:	Everybody's shaking hands, and I'm not getting any money!
GROUCHO:	I want to congratulate you for extricating me from this very embarrassing position, and I think you have thrown him a curve that will last him for some months.
	(Dwan exits.)

In fact, I had no idea what I was talking about. After his appearance on the show, Mr. Piffle had complained to Marion Pollock, who created the quiz questions. She took the case to Bernie Smith, who, as an old newspaper man, saw the possibility for some publicity. He set Piffle up to make his return appearance, and it was agreed that I would make the explanation, although no one knew what that would be. I called my brother, Dick, who had studied logic at the Jesuit University, Santa Clara. He told me about the syllogism with the undistributed middle and gave me the example of "all dogs are cats." My own background was in Economics at Stanford during the Depression. We studied the theory of business cycles and the principles of free-market economics, no training for any of the finer points of logic.

The gems most often had nothing to do with the script.

A French voice teacher attributed Groucho's addiction to cigars to the fact that, "As a baby, you were given the wrong kind of a bottle!"

"Mademoiselle," he replied, after a puff on his cigar, "I'll have you know I never had a bottle!"

An elderly woman who ran a boarding house for college students in Tennessee said she put the boys on the first floor and the girls on the second floor, but even so, "Sometimes I felt like using a broom."

"Why?" Groucho asked. "What was going on?"

"Oh," she said, "just different things."

"I didn't know there *were* any different things," Groucho said.

Another woman was describing a product she manufactured, a "magic pillow that wiggles and massages your feet."

"If I'm going to get something that wiggles," Groucho said, "I don't want a pillow. You may think you were describing a pillow. You were actually describing the girl of my dreams!"

Another time, he remarked to a pretty young woman, "You look very familiar to me. Have I ever been familiar with you?"

My personal favorite occurred sometime in the early '50s when a teenage girl named the young vocalist, Fabian, as her favorite singer.

GROUCHO: What does Fabian have that George Bernard Shaw doesn't have?

One evening he confronted a pair of young students, Carlos, from Franklin High School, and Nancy, from Eagle Rock High. Groucho asked each of them, "What grade are you in school?" The boy, Carlos, responded, "I'm a Junior B." The script took that subject no further, but when Groucho said, "A Junior B, eh?" there was a slight titter from the house. He decided to explore.

"Is that a small bee that hasn't gotten around to the flowers yet?" It was, in fact, a rather daring line for radio in 1949, when the birds and bees were still not subjects for open public discussion. In this case, I was able to persuade the censor that the image was sufficiently innocent to permit broadcasting.

Having an indication in the script of what the contestants were going to say gave Groucho a road map of the direction the conversation was intended to take. He would, therefore, not usually create any distracting tangents during these organized sequences. It was for that reason that he wrote several words on the cover sheet of his script every week for 16 years. The first words were "Line ahead," an admonition to be aware of

Groucho with Kuldip Rae Singh in his dressing room after the show, September 1956. Kuldip was a handsome young man with a wonderful singing voice. Bernie Smith brought him back on the program several times in the hope that he might be discovered by the movies or recording industry. It almost happened, but not quite. (Courtesy Paul Wesolowski)

what was coming next and not to go skittering down any comic blind alleys.

The second note was a single word, "Slow," intended to remind himself to take time to think. His cigar was a useful artifact in this maneuver. A slow, thoughtful puff on the Havana for the phrase to come full bloom—or, perhaps, to be rejected for another even better. When we were in England in 1965, doing the British version of the show, the staff and crew professed amazement at his slow pace, claiming that all their

comedians worked much faster, as did the Groucho of the movies, the much faster-talking Captain Spaulding or Dr. Hackenbush.

The third inscription was to remind him of one of his major comedy resources. It said, simply, "Fly off." When inspiration struck, he flew.

Finally, the fourth word was "Listen," perhaps the key to his whole technique.

There were also in the script two other cues, inserted by Bernie Smith. They were "PROD" and "FEU." "PROD" was simply a signal to Groucho to explore, that there might be more here than meets the eye.

"FEU" was an acronym for the common vulgarity that can be euphemistically translated as "foul 'em up." It was intended to produce the confusion routine. It was from the "FEU" passages that the best ad lib routines emerged.

A lovely example of the value of the "FEU" and of the way it functioned was in a conversation with a charming lady named Orpha Clinker, who had been an art student in Paris in the late 1920s. The script supplied Groucho with the leading question, "I've heard about those young art students in the Montmarte. What really went on?" (FEU).

Orpha recalled how she and a girlfriend entertained two sailors on shore leave. "We didn't have any cards or any way to entertain the boys, so we just sat on the floor and played tiddlywinks. It was around nine o'clock at night, and they'd been there about a half an hour, when...."

"You whipped out the tiddlywinks as soon as they got there?" Groucho asked. "Can you imagine these two guys just getting off the boat, and one says, 'Let's go see what we can pick up at the nearest bar.' And the other says, 'Are you crazy? Let's go over to her apartment, we're going to get some hot tiddlywinks!' So what happened? There you are, the four of you on the floor, playing tiddlywinks...."

"And the manager came up...."

"The manager? He wanted to get in the game, too?"

"No," Miss Clinker said, "he knocked on the door and said we were making too much noise...."

"You were making too much noise playing tiddlywinks? What were you playing with, loaded tiddlies?"

(Photofest)

As Long As They're Laughing

CHAPTER 5
The Frightened '50s

The life span of *You Bet Your Life* (1947-1961) comfortably embraced the decade of the 1950s. It was a time of picking up pieces and forming new patterns after the war, and a time of faceless foes and nameless fears. It was also a time when many social forces were simmering under a lid of largely self-imposed repression.

The sexual revolution was waiting to happen. The first laboratory tests on the birth control pill were done in 1951, but it was not until 1960 that the first oral contraceptive was approved for general use. The then notorious *Kinsey Report—Sexual Behavior in the Human Male* had been published in 1947, and *Sexual Behavior in the Human Female* followed in 1953, but both were usually treated as material to be received in a plain brown wrapper, and although they were widely and avidly read, the public reaction was a long series of cautious jokes. Just the mention of *The Kinsey Report* was good for a laugh in most venues.

The pressures were building in the 1950s, and some of them exploded in laughter in our studio. Often the trigger was not a calculated quip by Groucho but an innocently intended remark by a guest. In 1949, we paired Don McDuff, a young man engaged to be married, with Thelma Burroughs, a grandmother. Groucho asked Grandma Burroughs, "What's the most important advice you can give a young couple about to be married?"

Mrs. Burroughs replied, "I think they should have something in common and do things together, always."

The audience picked up even that slight innuendo and burst into laughter. Groucho waited a long time and then said, "You'll get nothing out of me on that one. We've been raided too often."

One of our guests in 1951 was a politician.

"What have you learned after 25 years in politics?"

"The old-fashioned way is still the best," he replied.

The audience leaped to the sexual interpretation and laughed for a full 15 seconds while Groucho waited, looking down. Finally, he held up his hand to stop the laughter. "I must have some kind of a reputation," he said. "There isn't anything anybody can say to me anymore that doesn't evoke some kind of a dirty laugh from the audience."

One evening in the early '50s, Groucho was in conversation with a young couple who were about to be married. The girl was pretty and demure, the boy handsome and very sincere. It had been an office romance, and they were still working across the hall from each other. Groucho asked a conventional question of the time, "Les, do you believe a woman should work after she's married?"

Les replied, "No, but I believe it's only right until we get a little money ahead in case of a sudden little—uh—mishap."

This was perfectly acceptable family comedy material, and the audience was delighted that Groucho waited for the laughter to die down. "That's certainly a new name for it—just what do you mean by that, Les?"

"Well, an emergency can come about," the young man replied. "Anything can arise."

The audience leaped on the word "arise," and the laughter exploded. Groucho didn't say anything incendiary—there was no need—but simply, "No, not anything," and let it go at that.

Essentially the same word sparked one of the longest continuous laugh sequences in the history of our show. Our guest was a slender, sharp-featured lady with a pleasant smile and a modest demeanor.

"A boarding-house keeper must have many curious experiences, Mrs. Lerner," Groucho said. "Do you have any hot ones you can tell us about?"

"Well, when we first got married, I thought I'd surprise my husband," the woman replied. "I decided I would bake him some rolls. So I put two yeast cakes in."

"In your husband?" Groucho asked.

That ludicrous but innocently intended suggestion from Groucho established the base for what followed, in spite of the fact that the woman replied, "In the rolls." She continued, "And then I put three more in, and I still couldn't get no rise out of 'um."

That did it. Laughter started, slowly at first, then spread. Groucho said nothing for 40 seconds. Finally, he held up his hand to stop the laughter momentarily. "Mrs. Lerner, before you arrived here, this was a perfectly innocent audience." What followed was two minutes and 15 seconds of almost continuous laughter. "Well, go on with the story. We're hellbent anyway. So you went to the store...."

"And I got five more yeast cakes," she said, "and still I couldn't get no rise out of 'um."

"He must have been around Mt. Whitney by this time," Groucho said.

"So I got so disgusted," Mrs. Lerner said, "I went and buried it in the back yard."

"Isn't that against the law?" Groucho said.

"I planted a geranium on top of it," she explained.

"That's a very interesting story, Mrs. Lerner...."

"I didn't finish it," she said.

"You certainly finished your husband."

By this time, some members of the audience were producing that peculiar moan that indicated delighted but helpless exhaustion. Mrs. Lerner did finish her story, which included a description of the whole mess rising from the ground with the geranium on top, but the audience had had enough by this time. It was an honest story, and innocently intended, but any mention of physical sexuality was, at that time, so carefully excluded, not only from the airwaves, but from polite conversation, that even this slight and obscure reference was enough to trigger the laugh.

I'm sure that the most mystified party to the occasion was Mrs. Lerner. It is doubtful that she had ever had such success as a raconteur, and she must have been especially baffled when her story, which had been such a smash in the studio, was not included in the broadcast. Some part of that show did have an after-life, however. Another television program, which did not have as responsive an audience as *You Bet Your Life*, called my partner, Bernie Smith, to ask if they could borrow that sound track to augment their studio audience laughter, and it subsequently made the rounds of several other programs. There was at that time—and perhaps still is—a skilled gentleman who possessed a machine containing tapes of a gamut of laughter. We never used his services on our show, relying

Sometimes Groucho's improvisational ways led him into traps without any help from anyone. (Courtesy Paul Wesolowski)

entirely on the studio audience, but he was employed by several situation comedies. He sat in the studio behind the scenes and supplied what was missing in audience reaction from chuckles to guffaws. Mrs. Lerner's yeast cakes saved many a show.

Sometimes Groucho's improvisational ways led him into traps without any help from anyone. Once, he was speaking to a woman who had just said that her husband was absolutely wonderful in every way.

"What does this Casanova look like?" Groucho asked.

"He's six-foot-five, 250 pounds of all man."

Groucho pondered the end of his cigar. There were a few semi-suppressed titters.

"What makes you think that just because a man is five inches taller than six feet that this makes him a man?"

There was a small yip from one female voice. Otherwise it was very quiet. The sense that 350 people were holding their breath was almost palpable.

"You know it doesn't go by size," Groucho continued. "A man's size has nothing to do with his ability in any way." There was dead silence.

"I'm trying to keep this on a euphemistic plane, and I question very much whether I'm succeeding."

The dam burst. After 20 seconds of full-throated laughter, both male and female, Groucho finally said, "I admit defeat."

By 1957, in our 11th year, the blue-noses were getting slightly more relaxed, or, perhaps, the censor that day was tired. At any rate, the following, which wouldn't cause a tremor today, was quite daring for its time and was actually broadcast. The guest, Gizelle D'Arc, was beautiful and from Paris, where she helped her mother run a restaurant.

"Can you cook?" Groucho wanted to know.

"Oh, yes."

"Can you imagine some fellow marrying this girl and finding out six months later that she can also cook?"

We were so afraid of words in the 1940s. In 1945, when I first came to Hollywood to work for the National Broadcasting Company, I was assigned to represent the network on the *Red Skelton Show*. One week, one of my duties was to make sure that Red did not utter the word "diaper" on his broadcast. I was instructed to order the engineer in the control booth to cut the program off the air if I detected that Red was starting the routine that required the use of that dreadful word. Fortunately, it was a dispensable joke, Red's producers decided to skip it, and the crisis never came to pass.

Today, 50 years later, I have just seen a re-run of that splendid program, *Picket Fences*, in which the words "orgasmic" and "ass" were an essential part of the plot development. In 1945, radio station licenses would have been revoked at the merest whisper of those words. And yet that episode of *Picket Fences* was a highly moral tale, developing a socially valuable message concerning sensitivity between men and women. It would not have been possible without the use of those words.

Groucho was not a dirty-word comedian. He refused to play Las Vegas, in spite of several lucrative offers, because he didn't want to use the kind of material that appealed to what he called "the saloon crowd." In fact, he didn't have any such material. He used a common four-letter word freely in his private conversation, but never, ever, onstage. It was, in fact, one of the first words I ever heard him utter. In 1947 John Guedel had called me and Bernie Smith to his then tiny office in the Taft Building in Hollywood to meet the star of our new show. Groucho must have been somewhat startled to see the youngsters who would be in charge of his destiny. I was 32, Smith and Guedel only a couple years older. His brother Gummo was with him, as usual, and someone brought up the question of Groucho's costume and makeup: Would he wear his frock coat and the painted mustache?

"Absolutely not."

"Even for publicity pictures?"

"No."

"The network won't like that," Gummo ventured.

"Fuck 'em," Groucho said. And that was that.

(Bernie Smith had a different recollection of his first meeting with Groucho. When he was introduced by John Guedel, Smith said to Groucho, "It's a great pleasure." Groucho said, "I've known him for years, and I can tell you, it's no pleasure.")

Women's liberation was still at least a decade and a half away.

Betty Friedan's ground-breaking book, *The Feminine Mystique*, would not be published until 1963. The bra burnings were a phenomenon of the '60s. The prototypical American married women were the faithful, cheerful, comfortable, and complacent mothers in *Leave it to Beaver, Father Knows Best,* and the Nelson family saga, *Ozzie & Harriet.* That's what everyone thought, or was supposed to think. *You Bet Your Life,* in this area too, reflected the climate of the times.

All married women were introduced on *You Bet Your Life* as housewives, and no one ever objected. Unmarried women were most often identified on the show as someone "who would like to get married but hasn't found the right mate yet," or, if they happened to be of a relatively advanced age, were called "old maids" or, later, in a minimally progressive step, "spinsters."

In April 1949, a young lady from Pasadena revealed that she was on the high-school debating team. Groucho proposed a debate and assigned her the affirmative case on the topic: "Resolved: Men Are Smarter than Women." She floundered a bit in meeting this sudden challenge, but did produce an argument based on the facts that men are the best professional chefs and that men produce all the money. In conclusion she said, "Girls, you'd better give up. It's a man's world." And there was general applause.

In February 1952, the contestants were a young woman who was an executive secretary with a concert management company. Her partner was a cab driver. At the start of the quiz, the cab driver, typically aggressive, took the ball and bet $19 of their $20 stake. Groucho said, "You didn't consult with Betty. Is this all right with you, Betty?"

"They always told me men handle the money. So I'll just go along with it." It turned out to be good judgment, since the cab driver knew what cities Greenwich Village, Basin Street, Nob Hill, and the Loop were located in, and they won $305, almost as much as it was possible to win at that time.

In March 1949, we paired an efficiency expert, a time and motion studies man, with a young married woman, introduced, of course, as a housewife. It was established that she had no children.The following, after the leading question, was improvised by Groucho. He asked the expert, "To be efficient, how many children should she have?"

MAN: Well, I would say that the average house has about a thousand square feet.

GROUCHO: That would be 500 children!

MAN: No, I'd say that each person should have about 200 square feet. So I'd say the average couple should have three children.

GROUCHO: Well, that's a curious way to get a family — go around measuring the floor. There must be a simpler procedure than that, I am sure.

I regret to report that the last sentence was censored, but it actually was a relative triumph of negotiation. I was able to persuade the authorities that "measuring the floor," by itself, had no carnal implications. It still boggles the mind to realize that we were not able to admit publicly in 1949 that there was, indeed, a simpler way of conceiving children.

The conversation continued with some material that was scripted.

GROUCHO: *(To the efficiency expert.)* One final question. What is the one big recommendation you could make to Mrs. Adamic?

MAN: Going up and down stairs is the worst thing women do. She should finish all her housework upstairs, then start on the ground floor. Don't keep going up and down stairs. That will tire you out more than anything else.

Grace Bradley and Groucho, after she used up almost the entire half hour talking during the February 1956 show. (Courtesy Paul Wesolowski)

GROUCHO:	Sounds like good advice. Mrs. Adamic, will you be sure to follow that advice?
WOMAN:	No.
GROUCHO:	This is mutiny! Why not?
WOMAN:	We haven't got an upstairs at our house.

The sequence worked fairly well but hardly seemed worth all the trouble. Today, we surely wouldn't construct a routine on the premise that a woman's chief concern was how efficiently she did her housework. In 1949, not only did Bernie and his writers create this passage, both Groucho and I reviewed it in the script and approved. And Mrs. Adamic, whatever she may think today, agreed in 1949 to go along with it.

In his remarkable book, *The Fifties* (Villard Books, NY, 1993, p. 272), David Halberstam points out that *I Love Lucy* was essentially an extended woman-driver joke. Lucy could do nothing right, never quite understood the true situation—gumming up the machinery in the candy factory, assuming ineffective disguises—she always got it wrong, until Desi forgave her in the end.[1]

In November 1948 our guest, selected from several we invited to attend the show, was a racing car driver, Mr. Joe Garson. His partner,

Mrs. Sheri May, was introduced as "a woman driver." Women were still rare enough as drivers to be considered a separate category. We certainly would not have introduced a male as "a man driver."

Groucho, with feigned confusion, said to Mrs. May, "You're a racing car driver?"

"Oh, no," Mrs. May replied, "I'm just a *woman* driver!"

"Mr. Garson," Groucho said, "as a race driver, which do you think make the better drivers, men or women?"

"Well," Mr. Garson replied, "I think, naturally, men make the best drivers."

"Why?" Groucho wanted to know.

"They seem to have better coordination and seem to watch the road better."

There was no audience reaction. Mr. Garson had apparently expressed the consensus.

In November 1950, we were still contributing our bit to the woman driver syndrome. We introduced a housewife and a driving instructor, and the following prepared conversation ensued:

GROUCHO: Let's see what you know about your car. For example, what's the carburetor?

WOMAN: It has something to do with the motor.

GROUCHO: That's right! You must be married to a mechanic! Where do you find the crankshaft?

WOMAN: We don't have one. We don't have to crank it.

Mrs. Housewife willingly lent herself to the charade, and we never had any doubt that she would.

In February 1958, we heard one faint indication that times were changing, that new standards might be emerging, this time in the field of popular music. Our guest was Mr. Truman Tomlin, who, as "Pinky" Tomlin, had been a popular band leader and song writer, with at least one big hit song in the late 1930s, "The Object of My Affections." I can remember in college days, pressing up to the bandstand in the Palm Court of the San Francisco Palace Hotel to hear him sing the familiar chorus for the sixth time in one evening. He obliged us on *You Bet Your Life,* of course, by singing his 25-year-old song to hearty applause.

Groucho said, "That song is as good today as it was 25 years ago, and a vast improvement over many of the songs that you hear now."

There was more vigorous applause, but, faintly in the background, there could be heard perhaps six young voices booing. The influence of Elvis was already being felt, and the Beatles were waiting just over the horizon.

In the area of race relations, we were a product of our times. In 1955, the same year that Rosa Parks refused to move to the back of the bus in Montgomery, Alabama, we finally paired a white woman and a black man. There was no slightest hint of any romantic linking; they just happened to have complementary occupations. The advertising agency heard about it in advance and raised a major fuss. I'm quite sure they never actually consulted the sponsor—the DeSoto division of Chrysler Corporation—on the matter. It was clearly part of their modus operandi to keep any hint of a problem from coming to the attention of the sponsor. But they predicted dire consequences springing from the predictable reaction of the Southern DeSoto-Plymouth dealers. Bernie Smith got stubborn. Backed by John Guedel and Groucho, he refused to change the booking. The show went on, there was a vociferous response from some Southern dealers, but no reprisals were taken. The show was doing too well in the ratings to risk losing it. We never repeated the experiment, however.

We can take pride in having been the first network program to include a black musician in our orchestra. At the same time, that man was the focus of a peculiar act of insensitivity.

When Groucho brought Jerry Fielding in as orchestra leader in 1949, we discovered that besides being a splendid musician who gave a real lift to the show through his music, he was also a fighter for causes. It bothered him that there were no black musicians at that time in any network program orchestras. There were, in fact, no black members of the motion picture studio orchestras. When it was necessary to show black musicians onscreen, in a night club scene, for instance, the black players were hired to appear on camera, but white musicians made the music.

When Fielding took over the *You Bet Your Life* band, he wanted to make a change in the instrumentation to include a musician who not only could double on saxophone and clarinet, but could also play flute.

He found the answer to that problem, and also the way to break the racial barrier, in the person of 23-year-old Buddy Collette. Buddy was ready for the challenge.

The brass and reeds of the orchestra. Back row, left to right: Ralph Fera, Maurie Harris and Seymour Shetlow (trumpets); Lloyd Ulyate (trombone). Front row, left to right: Joey Stablie (sax); Buddy Collette (sax); Hymie Gunkler (sax); Marty Berman (sax). Not shown: Tommy Romersa (drums); Milton Kesteubaum (bass).

"I felt like Jackie Robinson in the band," he says today.

After his stint in the Navy, Collette had used the G.I. Bill to study for four years with the best teachers in town. He emerged as a triple threat on clarinet, saxophone, and flute. And he shared Fielding's zeal for combating inequity.

At that time in Hollywood, there were two musicians' unions, Local 47 for whites, Local 767 for blacks. The result was an effective monopoly of the job market by the whites. There was no written rule against hiring a black musician for a studio orchestra. It just didn't happen. Collette and a group of friends, including the later renowned double bass player, Charles Mingus, were conducting a campaign to have a single union. To demonstrate that there were black musicians capable of playing any kind of music, they formed an interracial symphony orchestra. Jerry Fielding attended one of their concerts, heard Buddy Collette play the flute solo

Buddy Collette

in the Bizet "Carmen Suite." When Buddy demonstrated that he could also double on clarinet and saxophone, he was in.

In 1953 Collette and his friends did finally achieve their goal of an non-segregated union. Today, Buddy is on the Board of Directors of Local 47 and teaches music at Loyola-Marymount University.

As Long As They're Laughing

After Fielding left *You Bet Your Life,* a little ritual developed which I still look back on with embarrassment. Today, Buddy Collette says it happened accidentally, without any attempt to make him a figure of fun. But it continued as long as we did shows.

Part of our performance each week, before the actual program started, was an exercise known as "the warm up," designed to do just that to the studio audience. Groucho told some jokes, indulged in a string of outrageous remarks, and there was a series of ludicrous happenings, all designed to demonstrate to the audience that the point of the whole procedure was laughter.

At one point, Groucho introduced the orchestra, who appeared from backstage and paraded across an archway at the rear of the set while Groucho made a few mildly insulting remarks about their appearance and demeanor. One night, Buddy says, someone suggested that they parade around twice, "just to fool Groucho." So the 11 men crossed the archway, ran around backstage, and appeared again. When Buddy Collette showed up the second time, the audience laughed. Groucho didn't exploit the situation, merely said, "They breed like rabbits, these musicians," and let it go at that.

Today, Collette says, "It didn't bother me at all. I just kept laughing. People would say, 'How do you feel about that?' and I'd say 'About what?'" He felt secure, he says, "...with the guys in the band. I went to dinner with them at the Brown Derby in the rehearsal break, and there was never any problem. Of course, if I'd go to those places alone, it was a different story."

Still, the people laughed at the "double walk-around," and they laughed because Buddy was black. I remember feeling uneasy, but not uneasy enough to stop it, and nobody else, including Groucho, seemed to notice. After all, it got a laugh. There were still traces of the 1800s in the 1950s.

There were other areas in which the public conscience slumbered. In March 1955, one of our guests was Mr. Joe Weinstein, "world's largest feather merchant." He bought and sold feathers from many species of birds from all over the world, from ostrich to vulture. He did mention in passing that he could not use bird of paradise nor egret, but outside of that, there was no mention of conservation or preservation of endangered species, no negative reaction from the audience, and no critical mail. The time had not yet come.

In the 1950s, "gay" still meant "happily excited." Homosexuals were securely, if uncomfortably, locked in closets. The subject, the word, the fact, were not part of the public consciousness. In show business, the lisping, limp-wristed, "swish" character of Vaudeville had almost disappeared, but could still be seen in burlesque houses. On *You Bet Your Life,* when confronted with the reality, we, and our studio audience, simply pretended it wasn't there.

Our guest was a delicately handsome young man, blue eyes, blonde hair looking as though it had been artificially waved, almost a stereotype. The conversation revealed that he had turned down a job in a foreign country.

GROUCHO: Why did you turn down the job? Did you have a girl here, in this country, that you were enamored of?
MAN: No, I don't have a girl, Groucho.
GROUCHO: You don't have any girl?
MAN: No, sir. *(He smirked, slightly. The audience was very quiet.)*
GROUCHO: How old did you say you are?
MAN: Thirty-one.
GROUCHO: You've had a girl, I imagine.
MAN: How do you mean that?
GROUCHO: *(A slight pause. Silence in the audience.)*
            I mean it in the nicest way you possibly could.
            (There was a sense of tension relieved in the audience laughter. Groucho continued, playing by the conventional rules.)
            I mean, at some time in these 31 years, there must have been some girl you liked.
MAN: I liked traveling better, I'm afraid.
GROUCHO: I don't see the comparison, but—
            (There was a small laugh. He reached back for an old Vaudeville reference to get him out of it.)
            I know you need a bag when you travel, but I don't see....

The laughter was general, even for the strained joke, reacting to the vulgarism. The audience simply preferred to ignore any alternative reading of the situation. We lost the whole sequence to the censor, but only because of the use of the verboten word. Even in pre-women's-lib days, you were not allowed to call a woman a bag.

Part of the maturing of the American psyche took place during the quiz show scandal of 1957 to 1959. It was the moment of realization that everything you see on television ain't necessarily so.

During the '50s, the television set rapidly replaced the hearth as the focus of American family life. The entertainers who entered our homes by TV became familiars, welcomed almost as family members or, at least, as old friends. The contestants on quiz shows played a special role among these weekly guests. The program producers had discovered, almost accidentally, the value of home audience participation. It was, to some degree, more than a vicarious experience. The viewers actually played along with the contestants. Even if they missed a question, they were immediately given the correct answer so they could feel a little smarter than they were a moment ago. They identified with the players and triumphed when one of their favorites triumphed. It was that factor of favorites that was one of the two elements that led to the spectacular rise in the quiz shows' popularity and, eventually, to their downfall.

A feature of most of the quiz shows was the holdover, by which the winning contestant each week was held over to compete again, and again, until he or she was defeated. The producers shrewdly noticed that when an attractive and popular contestant was winning, ratings went up. The logical tactic, then, was to contrive somehow so that the personality kids were steady winners.

We were never guilty of the practice, primarily because we were only interested in people who were productive, interesting and funny for Groucho to talk to. If they could answer some quiz questions and make some money, that was fine, but that was not our primary objective.

The obvious way to be sure that your favorite contestant stayed on the show for several weeks, was to make sure he or she knew the answers to the quiz questions. Some of the quiz shows did just that. One of the simplest and most successful procedures was to give the contestants a sample quiz before the show. The preferred winners were then presented on the program with the questions they had answered correctly, and the designated losers were given questions they had missed. In the most notorious case in which someone finally blew the whistle, on the now famous *Twenty-One*, as dramatized in the film *Quiz Show,* the contestant who was cast as the villain claimed that he was pressured to answer incorrectly by the offer of a job which did not then materialize.

In the meantime, on *You Bet Your Life,* we blithely went our innocent way, securely holding our ratings position without the necessity of any hanky-panky. We had Groucho.

The other element in the quiz show ratings race was greed on the part of the producers, the contestants, and, vicariously, the audience. In lieu of entertainment, or, to be charitable, let us say in addition to entertainment, the programs offered the lure of very large sums of money. The $64 question became the $64,000 question. In 1958, Teddy Nadler (by then a household name) became the top prize-winner on the *$64,000 Challenge* with $252,000. But the balloon was about to burst.

Even though our ratings by then were suffering somewhat, we didn't try to compete, because we didn't have the budget for it. The total budget on *You Bet Your Life* of $47,500 per week was higher than any of the big-prize-money shows, but the money didn't go into prizes. Instead, it went, first, into the high cost of filming and then to Groucho. All the other quiz shows were live. Even so, according to Bernie Smith, who kept track of such things, in the first nine seasons of *You Bet Your Life,* on 3,041 shows, the contestants won $463,514. No one bothered to calculate the total for the entire 14 years.

At the height of the quiz craze, we did respond by changing the formula for the big question. In the tradition of the show, it was not done to the accompaniment of flashing lights and an electronic scoreboard. We brought in an old-fashioned carnival wheel for the contestants to spin. They picked a number. If the wheel stopped at that number, they won an additional $10,000. If it stopped on any other number, the prize was $1,000. The odds, never stated, were fairly large. It had no appreciable effect on the ratings.

In fact, I never thought of *You Bet Your Life* as a quiz show. Its appeal was comedy and the unpredictable, unique mind and style of Groucho. The quiz did serve a function in providing motivation for the contestants to appear, and it was useful for me in editing. If the interview was a disaster, I could include a few polite questions, delete all the rest, and cut to Groucho saying, "Now it's time to play *You Bet Your Life.*"

By 1957 and into 1958, there were signs that all was not well in the industry. An unsuccessful contestant on *The Big Surprise* sued, claiming fraud, and the Federal Trade Commission investigated briefly. One of the winners on the *$64,000 Challenge* told *Time* he knew his opponent had been cheated, but they didn't print it. Finally, in 1959, the whole thing exploded, and the shock wave damaged an innocent member of the

You Bet Your Life staff. The ultimate revelation concerned the nation's fair-haired contestant, Charles Van Doren, college professor, scion of a distinguished literary family, the winner of $138,000 on *Twenty Questions.*

Under accusations from a competitor, Van Doren had steadily insisted on his innocence, but finally, on November 9, 1959, bowing to the ponderous weight of the Subcommittee on Legislative Oversight of the House Committee on Interstate and Foreign Commerce, he told all. He said that the producer had given him the answers to the questions before the broadcast and had coached him how to act, not blurting out the facts, but appearing to struggle for the answer. Immediately, there were investigators at the offices and studios of every quiz program on the schedule. In snooping around *You Bet Your Life,* the FBI men found their antennae twitching when they encountered the case of William Peter Blatty, a young man who had once been a writer on one of John Guedel's shows and who later achieved worldwide fame as the author of the best-selling book and hit film, *The Exorcist.* He appeared on our show in disguise, pretending to be an Arabian sheik. He and his partner qualified for the big question and were asked, "Which of the seven wonders of the world is still in existence?" Mr. Blatty answered correctly, "The pyramid at Giza" and won $5,000. The FBI men said that question was too easy, especially in the light of its being asked of a former employee. Two investigators showed up at NBC an hour before a performance.

"Who wrote the question?" they wanted to know.

Groucho and I were busy onstage, but John and Bernie talked to them and, in the end, agreed to a sacrificial lamb for appearance's sake. In fact, it did seem to be a reasonable solution, and I probably would have agreed had I been in the meeting. But the person affected was deeply wounded.

Marion Pollock was a young divorcee in 1950, a single mother who needed a job. She had no professional experience but was very bright, and John put her to work searching for and interviewing potential contestants. In a short time, she absorbed the job of researching and writing the quiz questions. She worked alone with no double check except for a cursory review by John, Bernie, and me, who all had opinions about what was too hard or too easy. (If none of us knew the answer, it was too hard.) There was no board of review or academic authority in the studio during the show. If there was a dispute about an answer in performance, I made a snap judgment on stage, usually substituting another question and later

Arlene DiFraia with Groucho, February 1961. She and her partner, author William Peter Blatty, won $5,000 on the show. (Courtesy Paul Wesolowski)

editing out the one in dispute. There was never any serious question about the accuracy of Marion's facts during the entire run of the show.

In addition to writing the quiz, Marion continued to search for contestants and was also the last person to see them before they went onstage. She ushered them from their dressing rooms and held them in the sound lock until the secret word had been announced. It was that fact, that she had direct contact with the contestants and also created the quiz, that aroused the investigators' suspicions. So John and Bernie decided to eliminate even the appearance of the possibility of collusion and agreed that Ms. Pollock would no longer have contact with the contestants. Marion felt that she had been singled out as the one person on the staff who was a security risk and that her integrity had been challenged. The investigators were satisfied, however, and that was the end of the quiz scandal as far as we were concerned. Marion continued to write the quiz questions as long as we were on the air, and the experience, she said, helped her in what she undertook to do after *You Bet Your Life* went off the air. She had the most impressive post-show record of any of our alumni. Her experience in researching quiz questions prepared her for the scholastic grind when she returned to college and earned a Masters and a Doctorate in Health Education, became a full professor at Long Beach State University, and published five books. Tragically, her life ended in violence. She was attacked and brutally beaten in her home and died from the injuries in 1994.

As we moved into the '50s, there was a general unease in a helpless reaction to global events apparently beyond anyone's control. In 1948, the Berlin blockade was broken, but in 1949, the Russians exploded an atom bomb. In 1952, the U.S. conducted the first H-bomb test at Eniwetok, but in 1953 the Russians tested their H-bomb.

In February 1950, Senator Joseph McCarthy made his first speech claiming there were Communists in the State Department, Alger Hiss went to prison in 1951, and the icy fingers of McCarthyism reached out to touch *You Bet Your Life* in 1953. It was very direct and personal.

Groucho first met Jerry Fielding in 1949 when Jerry conducted the music for Groucho on a children's album called "The Funniest Song In the World" for Young People's Records. Jerry was then 23 and had been working professionally since he was 16 as an arranger for Kay Kayser and recently as conductor on the *Jack Paar Show,* the 1949 summer replacement for Jack Benny. He was an intense, handsome, slightly built young man of driving energy and enormous musical talent. Groucho was enthusiastic about his work and his personality and asked John Guedel to put him on *You Bet Your Life* as musical director starting with our third season in 1949. Jerry's resources far exceeded the demands of the show. He told Hector Arce in 1976, "The show was so easy it was like stealing money. It wasn't even work. But it was a big mention every week. In those days, everybody saw a hit show like that."[2]

In 1953, the House Un-American Activities Committee came to Hollywood. They had a list of Communist, "Communist front," "fellow traveling," or otherwise allegedly un-American organizations. Jerry told Arce, "There were 240 organizations on the Attorney General's list, and I belonged to at least 60 of them."[3]

Shortly after the committee set up shop in Los Angeles, Walter Winchell ran an item in his column stating that the committee was looking for Fielding because they had a subpoena out for him. By that time, Jerry had five radio shows and was doing a series of jazz concerts with our augmented band on Monday nights at the Crescendo nightclub, but somehow, according to Winchell, the subpoena servers couldn't find him. Some of the advertising agency people were concerned, but Groucho dismissed it as nonsense. The committee adjourned for the summer.

Then, one evening just after the start of our seventh season, while we were in the middle of a performance, two process servers slipped out of the wings to Jerry's podium and presented him with a subpoena to appear before the committee.

It was a very long wait to the end of the show. Then, Jerry says, "I took the thing... to Groucho and said, 'I quit. I'm saving you the trouble. Get yourself another fellow.' He said he wouldn't have that. He would not sit still for a political firing."[4]

But the powers at NBC were concerned. Especially when Jerry told them he intended to be an unfriendly witness, pleading the protection of the Fifth Amendment.

Jerry told me years later that what made NBC take the whole thing seriously was his suggestion that Groucho might somehow be vulnerable.

Groucho was certifiably liberal, certainly not a radical. He was not a joiner and generally did not lend his name to causes. Once, that I know of, in 1945, he endorsed a Hollywood committee organized to support liberal candidates and traveled to Seattle to a political rally. It was The Independent Citizens Committee of the Arts, Sciences & Professions, which disbanded its Hollywood chapter in 1946 but appeared on the Attorney General's list of subversive organizations in 1953, and Groucho had been a member.

Jerry's explanation to me was that he would not risk involving Groucho or any of his other friends. He said the rules of the committee were that if you testified to anything in your past, you were then required to tell everything or be held in contempt of Congress.

Left to right: Producer John Guedel, Orchestra Leader Jerry Fielding, Groucho, Director Robert Dwan, Mr. Guedel's Secretary Dorothy Nye, Announcer George Fenneman. The key player missing is head writer Bernie Smith.

At the hearing, he was asked, "Are you a member of the Communist Party?" He said no. Then he was asked, "Were you a member of the Party five minutes ago?" He took the Fifth Amendment. That's what was in the papers that night. "Fielding Takes Fifth. May have been Communist Five Minutes Ago."

There were frantic phone calls and meetings at a high level of which I was not a part. Finally, John Guedel called me on Tuesday morning and said I'd better call Jerry and tell him not to come in for the show Wednesday night. I called. Jerry sent his friend, Lynn Murray, a well-known Hollywood conductor, to cover for him that week. The next week we hired Jack Meakin to lead the band. Jerry never returned. He made only one request. "Please, protect the rest of the band." That was the condition I made to Meakin. No changes in the orchestra. "Keep all the guys."

Guedel says the Fielding firing was a direct order from the sponsor. They were vulnerable, as were the networks, the advertising agency,

Ed Tyler, Hy Freedman, Bernie Smith, Dorothy Nye, John Guedel, Groucho and I prepare for another show. (Courtesy Paul Wesolowski)

Groucho, John, and I. We were all vulnerable because everyone was vulnerable. The foe was faceless, something called public reaction. The weapon of the zealots was the threat of a boycott. The only possible response to that was defiance, and no one knew where that would lead. Would people stop buying DeSotos because Jerry Fielding took the Fifth Amendment? Would people stop watching *You Bet Your Life*? Probably not, but no one wanted to take a chance. There was no middle ground. I could have said, "If Jerry goes, I go." I didn't do it.

Jerry had a very hard time for a long while. I learned years later from Buddy Collette that the men in the orchestra contributed $25 a week each for almost a year to help Jerry out during the rough period. Finally his talent prevailed. Jerry was bitterly amused by the fact that when he was conducting a band in Las Vegas he was hired to conduct the orchestra for a series of radio programs sponsored by the Treasury Department in a campaign to sell U.S. Government Bonds. The shows toured military bases and other restricted locations. "It was okay for me to work for the United States Government, but not the Chrysler Corporation on a quiz show," he observed. He later wrote several film scores and was nominated twice for Academy Awards for his music for the motion pictures *The Wild Bunch* and *Straw Dogs*.

Years later, he came to a party at Groucho's house. I tried to tell him how I felt, and he was gentle and understanding—but he and Groucho never spoke.

The whole sorry affair is the one episode in the history of *You Bet Your Life* that I remember with regret, sorrow, and some shame.

Groucho and Marilee Jones promote the 14th season of *You Bet Your Life*. **I can't tell you what this had to do with the renewal of the show, but Groucho seems to be enjoying it. (Courtesy Paul Wesolowski)**

CHAPTER 6
The Cutting Room Floor

Let us return to the subject of sex. Groucho was, in fact, allowed a degree of sexual innuendo extraordinary for the times. It was part of his legend, italicized by the inimitable leer, pushing the limits of conventionality in the 1940s and 1950s, but gleefully accepted by a public teetering on the brink of the great sexual revolution.

The dirty old man image is still cherished by many. Last summer in Maine, a respectable New York dealer in rare books sidled up to me and said, conspiratorially, "Is it true Groucho made that crack about his cigar?" I knew immediately what he meant.

Early in the history of the show, one of our guests was a woman who had 20 children.

"Why do you have so many babies?" Groucho asked.

"I like children," the woman replied.

"I like my cigar," Groucho said, "but I take it out of my mouth now and then."

In an interview in *Esquire* in July 1972, Groucho insisted he never said it. For a long time, I, too, believed it was a figment of the mass libido. But, after discussions with my late partner, Bernie Smith, I am convinced that it did happen. I now believe that Groucho said it, but that he didn't mean what the dirty joke collectors think he meant. That remark, taken at its burlesque show level, was simply not his style. I'm sure he realized, as soon as he said it, that the fat was in the fire. The duration of the laugh that followed was proof.

But, outside of that studio audience and the 200 people who laughed that night, no one else ever heard that joke, because the exchange was never broadcast. It was never heard beyond the confines of NBC Studio C in Hollywood, and yet the story has spread to become an underground legend.

To round out an interview with a woman lawyer, Bernie contrived a "let's pretend" sequence in which the lawyer's client was accused of having robbed a bank on Hollywood Boulevard at three o'clock in the morning. Groucho was supposed to have been an eyewitness.

GROUCHO: Go ahead, shake my testimony. And while you're about it, let's see you shake your testimony.
(All of this set-up was written in the script. From here on, it was improvised by both parties.)

LAWYER: What were you doing on Hollywood Boulevard at 3 a.m.?

GROUCHO: I tried Sunset, and I wasn't having any luck over there.

LAWYER: Did you have a watch?

GROUCHO: Yes.

LAWYER: Did you make a note of the time?

GROUCHO: No.

LAWYER: Then how can you be sure what time it was?

GROUCHO: I looked at my watch, and it said a quarter to five, and when my watch says a quarter to five, it's three o'clock!

To my surprise, the Continuity Acceptance Department objected to that innocent invention. It was the Sunset Boulevard line that got us in trouble.

"What's wrong with the line?" I asked the censor, whom I shall call Mr. W. They came in varying degrees of rigidity. (Actually, they were all friendly, quite bright people, stuck in a miserable job.)

"Obviously, when he's talking about Sunset Boulevard, he's talking about hookers," Mr. W. said.

(Hookers were officially non-existent on radio in 1949.)

"Not necessarily," I said. "He could have been pushing drugs."

"That's worse," said Mr. W.

"Anyway," I continued, "the spectacle of Marx as a hooker is, to say the least, ludicrous."

"Let's not get into cross-dressing," Mr. W. said.

"Now you're really fantasizing," I said.

"Okay," said Mr. W., "what was he doing at 3 AM on Hollywood Boulevard?"

"Selling cheap watches," I said.

I knew I was going to lose from the beginning. A line merely had to *sound* illicit to be verboten in 1949.

In 1953, one of our guests was Irene Vezunis.

GROUCHO: When a fellow takes you home at night, does he say, "Good night, Irene?" (*A popular song of the day.*)
IRENE: It depends on the particular case.
GROUCHO: If he's real lucky, he doesn't say good night at all. (*Turning to me.*)
Clip, clip.

To a couple of newlyweds, he remarked, "Well, a new groom sleeps clean. That's a very old joke. Please ignore it."

Even that old folk-pun had to be ignored for the broadcast audience.

Groucho knew the rules, but he took the chances anyway, largely because he couldn't resist it.

In 1948, we were visited by Beria St. John, a housemother at the McKinley School for Boys.

GROUCHO: Do you have any children?
BERIA: There are a hundred and ninety-three.....
GROUCHO: A hundred and ninety-three! How long have you been married?
BERIA: At the McKinley Home, I mean.
GROUCHO: McKinley is home? Well, I should think he would be! I'll bet he never gets a night out! Do you drag him down to breakfast?

Mr. Louis Harrow appeared on the show on December 5, 1951. But this passage was only heard in the studio.

GROUCHO: Tell us about courtship in old Mexico. Did you ever get to go out alone together?
LOUIS: Yes, but her mother was a perfect chaperon, so we took her along with us.

GROUCHO:	And what happened?
LOUIS:	Well—five children.
GROUCHO:	When you went out on these dates, what did the chaperon do? Did she just curl up with a good book?
LOUIS:	No, she did the same thing we did.
GROUCHO:	You mean you have 10 kids now? I've stayed away from Mexico too long!

Sometimes Groucho didn't have to say anything, and we were still in trouble.

In December 1948, Miss Eleanor Way was introduced as a spinster.

GROUCHO:	Miss Way, what's the biggest mistake you ever made?
ELEANOR:	I went too many years with the wrong man.
GROUCHO:	How do you know if you didn't marry him?
ELEANOR:	Well, he had a boat, and he'd rather fiddle around with his old engine.... *(They laughed for 30 seconds while Groucho looked bemused, but no one ever heard it on the air.)*

I can't place all the responsibility on the censor, of course. I had a fairly blue nose, myself, in those days. The basic philosophy, shared by most producers in the 1950s, was that we should spare parents the embarrassment of answering questions like, "Why are they laughing, Daddy?" That this had a tendency to reduce comedy to the level of a six-year-old was, unfortunately, true. Mr. Marx's fertile mind did frequently create passages that might have been difficult to explain to the kiddies, and these were deleted without much argument.

One of our guests was identified as the manufacturer of products made from the fabric known as felt.

"What is felt used for?" Groucho asked him.

"Well, automobiles couldn't run without felt, the girls in California have that new look because of felt."

"You mean the girls couldn't run without felt?" Groucho asked. "A lot of them are felt and then run."

Groucho turned to me and said, "Hopeless!"

Another guest was a sculptor of ceramics.

GROUCHO:	How could you teach me?
SCULPTOR:	I could give you materials—a lump of clay.
GROUCHO:	What about the live model you mentioned?
SCULPTOR:	I could arrange that.
GROUCHO:	That would be good, I think. What else?
SCULPTOR:	A lump of clay and a sharpened stick....
GROUCHO:	You give me that live model and a stick, and I'll do my own business.

The image was too vivid for all concerned, and out it went.

A woman married to a Marine was being interviewed. Groucho asked her to describe her husband.

WOMAN:	Oh, he's really gung ho.
GROUCHO:	What is gung ho? Does that mean he works at a Chinese laundry?
WOMAN:	No, Groucho, gung ho means he's all Marine.
GROUCHO:	Are you sure your husband hasn't lost some of his buttons at this laundry?
WOMAN:	I don't think he ever lost his buttons at the laundry, but he lost his pants at the wedding.
GROUCHO:	That's a little premature, isn't it? *(After the laugh subsides.)* Well, tell us about some other experiences that we can conceivably use here tonight.
WOMAN:	I answered a newspaper ad a while ago. A gentleman in Laguna Beach....
GROUCHO:	There are no gentlemen in Laguna Beach.
WOMAN:	No, this gentleman is now abroad. *(Groucho employs a very subtle eyebrow.)*
GROUCHO:	This couldn't be Christine, eh? *(In the '50s, Christine Jorgenson was notorious for having undergone a sex-change operation in Denmark.)*

The entire passage landed on the cutting room floor.

We didn't edit only to protect the proprieties or to placate the censor; sometimes it was to protect Groucho himself, from himself. We trod a narrow line between dulling the cutting edge of his personality and

Sometimes cuts were made to protect Groucho from himself. (Courtesy Paul Wesolowski)

preventing him from being universally disliked for being outrageously rude. We were always aware that many people found him abrasive or "too rough on the contestants and that nice George Fenneman." In pursuit of the mass audience, we sought to avoid the image of "the mean old man."

His guest one evening was a short, plump, sharp-featured woman who ran a boarding house.

"What do you serve in this hash-house?"

"Not hash," she replied. "Chicken. Everyone likes chicken, so that's what we serve. Sometimes I think I'll turn into a chicken."

Groucho looked at her over the top of his glasses. "Well, Margaret, you don't have far to go."

The audience laughed, but there were some gasps and a few murmurs. The woman forced a smile. We decided it was too rough.

One of our favorite contestants was a very sweet but decidedly unglamorous lady named Anna Badovinac. Her interview was so successful, in fact, that she was the first guest we invited back for a second appearance. As briefly as possible, her story was this: She was born in a town called Badovinac, in Yugoslavia. Everyone in the town, she said, was named Badovinac. She was married to a man named Badovinac for 12 years and then to a second man named Badovinac for 30 years. Badovinac #1 left her to come to the United States. She followed and found he was living with Badovinac #2, but when he heard she was coming, #1 left. Anna got a divorce from Badovinac #1 and married Badovinac #2, with whom she had eight children.

GROUCHO: The name of this story is Anna and the King of Badovinac. How are you making out with Badovinac #2?
ANNA: He died three years ago.
GROUCHO: I'm very sorry to hear that, Anna. Maybe he's not dead, maybe he's just hiding.

There was a sort of shocked laugh. Groucho tried, unsuccessfully, to soften the blow.

"I'm sorry he's dead, Anna, but he certainly knew what he was doing."

This, incidentally, was one of the rare occasions that I'm aware of when Groucho incorporated a line from one of his old films into his *You Bet Your Life* improvisations. "How do you know he's dead, maybe he's hiding" is adapted from a line to Margaret Dumont in *Duck Soup*.

Editing sometimes resulted in some baffling product. Often it made Groucho's mind appear to have some peculiar limitations when he apparently refused to pursue what seemed to be interesting lines of investigation. Many times, when the guests were encouraged to talk freely, the result was interesting, but not funny, and funny was the criterion.

In April 1959, one contestant revealed that he had flown an airmail plane from Mexico City to Tampico, had done pearl diving off Baja, California, and had fought over 200 bulls. Groucho did, of course, in

Timely Topic—Groucho Marx and model Marianne Gaba spell out the news that *You Bet Your Life* moves to a new time slot on the NBC-TV network this fall. Starting Thursday, Sept. 25, Groucho will be seen two hours later than in previous seasons. (Original caption, 8/15/58) (Photofest)

performance, ask the man about his experiences as a pilot, a pearl diver, and a bull fighter, but nothing comedic developed, so it all disappeared in the editing as if it had never happened. In desperation, I included in the final version the one prepared joke that got any reaction. "You've met over 200 bulls?" Groucho asked. "You must be the envy of every cow in Mexico." When that was the high point of the interview, it cannot be listed among our triumphs. The other guest, however, was a young woman who really had nothing to say, but said it funny. She told a very ordinary story of how she met her husband, but she remembered and recounted every detail of the courtship, including the day, date, and time of every development in the romance. With Groucho's help, that got pretty funny and was largely preserved in the broadcast.

In February 1954, our guest was Robert Reuben, who was then the proprietor of The Pen and Quill, a reputable restaurant in Manhattan Beach, California. He told an amusing story about a Halloween holdup at his restaurant in which the bandits wore masks. But everyone else was wearing masks, too, so no one would take the thieves seriously. That story worked fine. But in performance, Mr. Reuben also told of his career as a foreign correspondent. He had parachuted into Normandy the day before the invasion, he had spent a year at the South Pole with Admiral Byrd, had met Churchill, Roosevelt, Eisenhower, and Chiang Kai- Shek. He had a story about Eleanor Roosevelt being kind and motherly when he was ill, and stories about the liberation of Paris and the signing of the Peace Treaty after the Pacific War. Ridiculous as it seems from this perspective, all that was deleted from the broadcast in favor of the Halloween story. Sometimes I'd like a chance to go back and do it again.

The case that still embarrasses me is that of my friend, Ray Bradbury, who appeared on the program in 1956 when he had written the screenplay for *Moby Dick*. On the broadcast, that fact was established, and Ray admitted that he had written some books, but that was all. Surely, a wasted resource. I wrote to Ray recently to ask him what his reaction was to the broadcast, and all he remembered was that he had missed the big question in the quiz. The question was, "The film *The Heiress* was based on a novel by Henry James. Name the novel."

"*Washington Square,* of course," Bradbury wrote me in reply. "I knew the answer, but froze, losing a thousand dollars!"

In spite of all that, I have never considered the editing function to have been negative. Its most important purpose was to free Groucho to take chances, to experiment, try alternatives and, often, strike gold. Improvisation, of all the arts, requires the freedom to fail without penalty.

For example, one evening his guests were a couple of high school students. He asked Carlos, age 16, what he wanted to do when he left school.

CARLOS	I'd like to make money.
GROUCHO:	You mean you'd like to be a counterfeiter? For graduation, I'll give you one of my old printing presses. *(All of that was in the script. Then Groucho pushed a little further.)*
GROUCHO:	What does your father do? Is he a counterfeiter, too?
CARLOS:	Oh, no, he's a printer. *(The audience was amused by the coincidence. Groucho decided to explore a tangent.)*
GROUCHO:	They call them counterfeiters here, but in France, where they pass counterfeit francs, they call them frankfurters. *(There was a smatter of polite laughter. Groucho turned to where I was standing off camera, made a scissoring gesture with his fingers and said, "Clip, clip." No laughter, no joke.)*

On the evening of March 31, 1949, Fenneman had just finished delivering a commercial for Elgin American Compacts. The orchestra was in the midst of the customary musical "button." Groucho suddenly shouted, "Stop the music! Stop the music!" The music came to a ragged stop on the unexpected cue. Those who were startled included not only the conductor, Jerry Fielding, and the members of the orchestra, but John Guedel, Bernie Smith, the engineer, the audience, Fenneman, and me. We all waited expectantly. ("Stop the Music" was a big-money musical quiz popular on radio in the late 1940s. When a correct answer was received, the M.C., Bert Parks, shouted, "Stop the music!" and the phrase became part of the popular parlance.)

When all was quiet, Groucho said, "I didn't have anything to say. I just wanted to see if it would work!"

That bit was broadcast as performed.

The taping or filming of *You Bet Your Life* also allowed contestants to talk freely. Sometimes, the humor sprang from their talking and talking and talking. Most people are not very skilled at telling a story economically, so what might have been a normal dissertation in casual conversation seemed much longer on a television program with the whole nation watching.

My problem in editing was what faces every filmmaker or dramatist who wants to depict boredom without making it boring. In my case, I had the help of the studio audience, who, in a minute or so, would begin

As Long As They're Laughing

to appreciate the situation, usually encouraged by some visual cues from Groucho. He merely had to look over the top of his glasses with a mildly bemused expression to convey his state of mind.

One quite charming and attractive woman responded to the standard question, "How did you meet your husband?" with an explanation of her background as a student nurse, a description of the appearance and character of her overbearing supervisor, and a detailed setting of the scene in the New York city morgue where she had gone against regulations with a friend and accidentally encountered a young man.

"Was he dead?" Groucho asked.

"I thought he was," she said, and continued the story.

After a minute and a half, the audience began to appreciate the situation. At two and a half minutes of non-stop narrative, Groucho said, "This is something like *Gone With the Wind*. Could you *Readers Digest* this just a little bit?"

She continued unabashed. At three and a half minutes, with the denouement apparently nowhere in sight, Groucho said, "I can see why you only had two children, Mrs. Tynan. There just wasn't time for any more." The woman, I must submit, did not seem at all offended, but rather pleased with her performance, interpreting the laughter, I suppose, as an appreciation of her story.

(The broadcast version lasted a little over a minute and a half, just about long enough, I hoped, to make it seem almost too long.)

Another function of editing, of course, was to trim out all those jokes, written or improvised, which turned out not to be jokes. We had a jury of 500 people ready to give an instant verdict.

Sometimes the zeal of our writers in looking for every possible chance for humor exceeded their judgment.

Our guest was a young Chinese student who later demonstrated that he did a pretty funny Groucho imitation.

The script read this way:

GROUCHO:	You're James Hong? Where are you from, Jim?
HONG:	I'm from Minnesota.
GROUCHO:	I thought so. Hong is a fine old Scandinavian name. Are you any relation to my uncle?
HONG:	No, I don't think so.
GROUCHO:	I just wondered. I had an uncle once who was hong. I don't know why, all he did was steal horses. He was

Many of our contestants were from foreign countries. Here some of them pose with the flags of their homelands.

so crooked, he always stole out of a room. *(Audience groan.)* Does Hong have any particular meaning in Chinese?

As the program matured, the writers relied less and less on these formulaic "uncle" jokes, usually involving "my Uncle Julius." We all learned, slowly, that the comedy worked best when it sprang from the personalities and experiences of the contestants. In this case, the audience verdict was clear.

When the show was broadcast, six weeks later, the dialogue was heard this way:

GROUCHO: You're James Hong? Where are you from, Jim?
HONG: I'm from Minnesota.
GROUCHO: Does Hong have any particular meaning in Chinese?

James then explained that his family name was Ng, but that was too hard for Americans to pronounce. Groucho tried to pronounce it anyway. Silly, but big laughs. Then Groucho constructed a little routine on the spur of the moment.

GROUCHO: Do you speak Chinese?

HONG: Yes, we speak it at home quite often, so I have to know it.

GROUCHO: Could you say, "Mother, give me a salami sandwich?"

HONG: We don't eat salami.

GROUCHO: Well, could you say, "Mother, how is the chow mein tonight?"

HONG: *(He does, in Chinese.)*

GROUCHO: She says n.g. and that's the finish of that meal. And you go out and get a salami sandwich.

It was a tricky process none the less. I deleted from the broadcasts many passages in which contestants made statements that I knew were honest and true, simply because they were not credible, sounding too glib or outlandish. I certainly caused pain to my partner, Bernie Smith, although he rarely complained. John Guedel and Groucho did grumble on occasion, but they never tried to overrule me. My defense was that a phony-sounding passage, true or not, cast doubt on the validity of everything else we did.

These were highly subjective judgments, however, and I was often swayed to accept some edgy material because it led to a successful Groucho line. Another high school boy, Jimmy, had told him that the latest fad in school was "be-bop" talk.

"What do you say when you see a cute little chick?" Groucho asked.

"Be-bop shebang," Jimmy said.

"Be-bop shebang?" Groucho repeated. "That means he's got a cottage up in the country, a small shebang someplace?"

I thought that was so inventive, especially since it was an ad lib by Groucho, and it got such a good laugh, that I ignored the somewhat suspect validity of the boy's be-bop talk, and the whole thing was broadcast.

My most concise, and memorable, lesson on editing came one day in 1958 when Groucho took me with him to visit George S. Kaufman in his New York apartment. For me, it had the aura of a visit to a tall, thin guru. I remember his being seated in a chair with his long legs seeming to be entwined at least twice around each other.

Discussing business with Gummo (left) and Groucho (right) in his dressing room after a performance. (Courtesy Paul Wesolowski)

"Here's a young director, " Groucho said. "Tell him how to direct."

"Well," Mr. Kaufman said, "if you have a script, and it says, 'Sit down, I want to talk to you,' cut that out."

End of instruction.

Applied to *You Bet Your Life*, it meant trimming out all the little stuttering fumbles, pauses, and hesitations, the groping and probing down blind alleys that are part of any ordinary conversation, and turning the passage into a piece of entertainment.

As an example, our guests one evening were Miss Gross, in charge of fan mail at Universal Studios, and Miss Ring, president of the Dana Andrews fan club. Groucho spoke first to Miss Ring.

GROUCHO: What fan club are you president of?
MISS RING: The Dana Andrews fan club.

GROUCHO:	Mm, hmm. How many members do you have?
MISS RING:	Uh, oh....
GROUCHO:	Nationally, I mean.
MISS RING:	Nine hundred, nationally.
GROUCHO:	Nine hundred. Mm, hmm. Why did....
MISS RING:	A hundred and fifty here in Los Angeles.
GROUCHO:	Uh, huh. Why did you pick Dana Andrews? Why didn't you join the Groucho Marx fan club?
MISS RING:	I didn't know there was one.
GROUCHO:	I'm not sure there's a Groucho Marx. The fact is, I have a very devoted fan club, Barbara. They send me thousands of letters every month. Credit managers all over the country belong to it.

As broadcast:

GROUCHO:	What fan club are you president of?
MISS RING:	The Dana Andrews fan club.
GROUCHO:	How many members do you have?
MISS RING:	Nine hundred, nationally.
GROUCHO:	Why did you pick Dana Andrews? Why didn't you join the Groucho Marx fan club.
MISS RING:	I didn't know there was one.
GROUCHO:	I'm not sure there's a Groucho Marx.

(In performance, he turned to the other guest.)

GROUCHO:	Miss Gross, what's the oddest letter you ever got from a movie fan?
MISS GROSS:	Well, I think the woman who had seen the *Life of Riley*.
GROUCHO:	She had seen the whole life of Riley or just....
MISS GROSS:	She had seen the movie.
GROUCHO:	Oh, just the movie.
MISS GROSS:	Yes. She asked for William Bendix. If we would send him. She sent $10 to cover the charges.
GROUCHO:	And he wouldn't go.
MISS GROSS:	No, he told us to send back the $10 and send a big picture that he autographed to her personally.

The cast and crew of *You Bet Your Life*

GROUCHO:	I listened to Benny Goodman last night, and he sent me.
MISS GROSS:	And then we have the young chap, oh, this probably happened a couple of years ago who wrote in and asked for one of our star's, shall we say, unmentionables. He was making a hobby of collecting them.
GROUCHO:	Let's not say unmentionables. Let's keep this within reasonable confines. Lingerie, eh?
MISS GROSS:	Well, yes, and he said he was collecting them. It was a hobby. He had over a hundred.
GROUCHO:	He was collecting them? Filled or empty?
MISS GROSS:	He didn't say.
GROUCHO:	He didn't say whether he wanted them on the half-shell or not.

Edited version, as broadcast:

GROUCHO:	Miss Gross, what's the oddest letter you ever got from a movie fan?
MISS GROSS:	Well, I think the young chap who wrote in and asked for one of our star's, shall we say, unmentionables

As Long As They're Laughing

Groucho and the duck share a special Emmy in 1975. The medal he is proudly wearing is the French Commander *des Arts et Letters* **awarded to him by the French government.**

GROUCHO: Let's not say unmentionables. Lingerie, eh?

MISS GROSS: Well, yes. He said he was collecting them.

GROUCHO: He was collecting them? Filled or empty?

Incidentally, the reference to George S. Kaufman a few moments ago reminds me of a remark by Groucho during one of the periods when he was single:

> All I want is a girl who looks like Marilyn Monroe and talks like George S. Kaufman.

Groucho with the curator of Grant's Tomb. (Courtesy Paul Wesolowski)

As Long As They're Laughing

CHAPTER 7
Who's Buried in Grant's Tomb?

Groucho was no Alex Trebek, and his supporting troops were not organized like the production staff of *Jeopardy!* He had no panel of experts sitting off camera to check every answer and come up with clarifications or corrections. One of our first rules was that the contestants agree on a single answer, but although Groucho repeated the rule three times during each broadcast, he rarely enforced it. Usually, as soon as he heard a correct answer from one of the pair, he said "Right!" and that was it. Of course, when one of them gave an answer and Groucho didn't immediately say "Right!" they knew that response was probably wrong and could search for another one.

On April 7, 1954, Mrs. Ruth Wood, "a housewife," and Mr. Fred Heaton, "a man from the Gas Company," were given the question, "What is a broad waistband worn in place of a vest with men's dress clothes?" She said "cummerbund," he said "bandalero" very firmly and definitively. Groucho said, "Get together." They did not negotiate. The bell rang. Groucho said, "She said it, and I'm not going to take anything else. It's cummerbund."

Unfortunately, they did not have even a single answer for, "What is vainglorious or exaggerated patriotism?" So, lacking any chauvinism, even in their vocabulary, they went away with $80.

Groucho was also extremely flexible in his interpretation of what constituted a correct answer. "Pasteur," he ruled, was close enough to "pasteurization," and since "debutante" contained the expected word "debut," it was also acceptable. He decided that "Mogenot Line" was close enough to "Maginot Line" and that "infinite" was a reasonable alternate for "ad infinitum."

I can recall only one case in which Groucho deliberately helped the contestants. They were Ted and Tom LeGarde, twin brothers from Australia, originally cowboys from the outback, now itinerant entertainers, in Hollywood to try to break into the movies. They sang Australian songs, did bird imitations, and spectacular tricks with a bullwhip. As the climax to their interview, they proposed to use the bullwhip to remove a cigarette from between George Fenneman's lips. Even George was not sure until the very last moment that they would not actually attempt it—a great test of George's faith in our ultimate good sense.

When it came to the quiz, the twins chose "Professions of Famous People," and it quickly became apparent that charming as they were and skillful as they were with the bullwhip, they were not fonts of knowledge.

That season (1957), the challenge was to give four correct answers in a row to win $1,000. Two incorrect answers in a row, and they were finished. I did not like the format because it was possible for the quiz to take an inordinate amount of time if they kept alternating between right and wrong answers, thereby digging into the time available for comedy. Marion Pollock, who prepared the questions, was not fond of it either since she had to prepare a very long list of possible questions.

On their first question, the boys could not identify Chester W. Nimitz as an Admiral. (This was not very long after the war, remember.) They did take a stab and tagged the then well-known performer, George Arliss, as an actor. They did not know that Sir Arthur Sullivan was a composer. One wrong again. One more wrong, and they were finished. "What was Paderewski's profession?" They said, "Composer." Paderewski was, indeed, a composer, although he was primarily known as a great pianist. So Groucho said, "Right."

Groucho then said, "You boys are making me nervous. I'll find something on here you can answer." Then, out of his head, he said, "Who was Les Darcy?"

"A fighter," Tom said immediately.

"From where?" Groucho asked.

"Australia," they both said together.

"Right!"

So they had two right.

"Name the capitol of Australia."

"Canberra!" they shouted.

There were cheers.

"You now have three right!" Fenneman announced.

But that was as far as even Groucho could go. They did not know the occupation of Frank Lloyd Wright, and they thought Vincent Van Gogh was probably a scientist. They were finished.

"For $25," Groucho said, "what baby animal lives in a pouch?"

"Kangaroo!" they said, and left relatively happy.

Our original quiz, which embodied the concept in the title, *You Bet Your Life*, and which we maintained for six years, was relatively simple and clear, and I preferred it to the variants. But it did have one serious flaw. Too many people went broke.

The rules were simple, and Fenneman could explain them in a few sentences. "Each of our couples has $20. They bet as much of their money as they want on each of four questions. The couple that earns the most money gets a chance at the big question at the end of the show."

Typically, they would bet $10 on their first question. If right, they had $30. They would bet all but five of their stake on the next three questions for a grand total of $105. If they missed the last question, they would close out with five dollars, and Groucho would ask them, "Who is buried in Grant's Tomb?" for an additional $25 to split between them.

As time went on, contestants became aware of the importance of accumulating as large a stake as possible but still protecting themselves from going broke. A frequent pattern became to bet all but a few cents on each question. If they withheld a penny each time, they could accumulate $319.85 with four correct answers. If they missed the last question, they had a penny, which still might qualify for the big question if the other two couples went broke. That did happen on several occasions. (The Grant's Tomb money didn't count in qualifying for the big question.)

On December 3, 1952, our first guests were Mrs. Natalie Spofford, a forelady in a laundry, and Mr. Rudolph Florentino, who once worked as a double for Rudolph Valentino in the movie *Son of the Shiek*.

"Rudolph Florentino," Groucho said. "That's a very euphonious name. I might say that's about the [most] euphonious name I've come across in a long time." They selected the category "Words Taken from Names," bet all but two dollars on the first three questions, got them right, and had $146 in their stake going into the last question. They bet it all.

"A long dagger-shaped knife was named for its designer, an American frontiersman. What is the name of the knife?" The closest they could come was "jack knife."

"Sorry, it's Bowie knife."

"And you've lost all your money," Fenneman proclaimed.

"What color are the blue bells of Scotland?" Groucho asked. And they retired with $25.

This happy couple has to answer one more question to win $5,000.

The next couple was Marie Clark Miller, a poet, and Maurice Wolfson, a building wrecker. Mrs. Miller quite logically selected famous poems as their category, but, as sometimes happened, she froze in the quiz. She knew Poe composed *The Raven*, and they had $35. They bet $30, but she could not come up with Joyce Kilmer as the author of *Trees*, so they had five dollars. They bet it all, but Marie could not connect Walt Whitman with *O Captain, My Captain*. They got the Grant's Tomb treatment and retired, crestfallen.

As Long As They're Laughing

Our third pair of guests was a delightful young couple from Scotland, Mr. and Mrs. John Robert Sweeney. They selected famous ships as their category, bet $19.97 on their first question and knew that the *Merrimac* fought against the *Monitor*. They bet all but two cents again and correctly identified the *Santa Maria* as one of Columbus' ships. They only withheld one cent on the third question and scored with the *Titanic*. They had $159.83 and bet it all.

"What U.S. battleship was sunk in Havana harbor during the Spanish-American War?"

Unfortunately, "Remember the *Maine*" was not part of Scottish folklore, and they lost it all.

"What do you brew in a teapot?" got them a consolation prize of $25.

Fenneman said, "Groucho, all of our couples tonight lost all their money, and that means that all three couples will be back in just one minute to get the chance at the $2,500 question."

This involved some scrambling in the camera department. Since the cameras were not on wheels, and zoom lenses had not yet been developed, we had to change lenses on three of the cameras to accommodate the larger than usual crowd on stage. That having been accomplished, the three pairs of contestants were brought back to the stage. Each had been given a small card and a pencil. Each pair was to write a single answer, and if all three were right, they would divide the $2,500 between them.

"From 1907 until 1916," Groucho said, "an eccentric monk exerted a powerful influence over the court of Russia. His power was ended when he was assassinated by a group of nobles. For two thousand, five hundred dollars, by what name do we know this man?"

Marie, the poet, immediately shouted, "Rasputin!"

"Write it down," Groucho said.

The music played for 15 seconds, George collected the cards and handed them to Groucho. To no one's surprise, they all said, "Rasputin."

"Rasputin is right," Groucho said. "You all had the right answer, so you each win $833.33!"

I was impressed then, and still am, that Groucho did the arithmetic in his head.

That was the closest we came to a complete wipe-out until October 21, 1953. The big question that night was worth $4,000. Our first guests were Mrs. Gretchen Alpert, a constable, and Mr. Fortune Gordine, world's

Groucho checks out an NBC camera in this obviously posed publicity shot. We never used television cameras on the show, only film cameras and Groucho never displayed any interest at all in the cameras! (Photofest)

record holder in the discus throw. They selected "The Animal Kingdom" as their category and built their $20 to $160 by identifying breeds of dogs, sheep, and lizards. They bet it all on the fourth question but did not know that "sperms, sulfur bottoms, and bottle-noses" are whales.

"How many shots in a six-shooter?" got them a $25 consolation prize.

Mrs. Lorena Nelson and Mr. Robert Disterdick were next. She was in the ladies' wardrobe department at Twentieth Century-Fox, and he was an executive assistant in the Los Angeles probation department. Their category was "English Expressions for American Words." They knew a tram is a streetcar, bet all of their $40 on the next question, did not know that an iron monger is a hardware store, and were broke.

"How many wheels on a tricycle?" gave them the $25 "Grant's Tomb" prize.

The final couple to try for the $4,000 was Mary Campbell, a dress shop operator, and a schoolboy, Leonard Ross, who was a mathematical wizard. They selected "Canadian Cities and Provinces" and again, perhaps spurred by the size of the big money at the close, bet all their stake on every question. They knew Montreal is in Quebec and Halifax in Nova Scotia, but thought Gander was in Saskatchewan instead of Newfoundland. They were broke. "What Shakespearean character gives *Hamlet*'s soliloquy?" gave them $25.

So, once again, Fenneman announced, "All three couples lost all their money, so all three get a chance at the $4,000 question!" And once again, all three couples appeared on stage with cards and pencils to write down their answers.

"The present calendar is named for the Pope who introduced it. For $4,000, what do we call our present calendar?"

The music played for 15 seconds, but it was not long enough. No one knew the answer. They all went away with their $25 consolation prizes.

That was the last straw for John Guedel. During the performances, John always sat on some steps in a hallway outside of the control booth. He did not like to sit in the control room because of all the distracting chatter and second-guessing from the coterie of V.I.P.s and visitors. John was not a man given to verbal profanity. His way of expressing his frustration was to break lead pencils in half. That night he broke six pencils. The next week, we had a different quiz in which no one could go broke. Under the new format, Groucho had a list of 10 questions, weighted according to value and difficulty, ranging from an easy question for $10 to a fairly difficult one for $100. In its most refined form under this system,

Groucho wasn't always consistent in observing his prejudice against "people in funny hats." When you are doing publicity photos, you sometimes get desperate. (Photofest)

the couple was given a $100 stake to start. They selected four questions of any value from 10 to 100 and won the value of the question for a correct answer. If they were wrong, they lost half of whatever stake they had at the time. Even if they should miss all four questions, they still would close out with $6.25. But that never happened. They always could answer at least the $10 question. The format worked pretty well for several years until John got restless and invented another one.

Our most unusual quiz session occurred in 1958, in the middle of our 11th year, and started with a special appearance by the world-renowned bridge expert and author, Charles Goren.

When greeting Mr. Goren, Groucho, for no reason, said, "Do you mind if I call you Jake?"

"Not at all," Goren replied, "but I might respond better if you called me Charles, since that's my name."

There was a trumpet call, the band played "The Stars and Stripes," the duck descended from his perch above, and Mr. Goren and his partner each received $50 for his having said "name," the secret word. The interview then proceeded well, with Mr. Goren, among other things, telling of being invited backstage during the Broadway run of *I'll Say She Is* to teach the Marx Brothers how to play bridge. He started the lesson by saying that the game is played with a deck of 52 cards. "Groucho stood up, said that was as much as he could absorb in one session, and left."

When it came time to play our game, Mr. Goren said, "I'd like to check out and give my place to some deserving young man who'd like to improve his state in life."

GROUCHO: Is there a deserving young man in the audience?
            (No volunteers.)
            Is there a sailor or a soldier who can come up here and pinch hit?
            Apparently not.

            (Before the show had started, Groucho had introduced the then rising young comedian, Ernie Kovacs, who was seated in the audience.)
GROUCHO: Come on, Kovacs, get on your feet.
            (Applause.)
GROUCHO: *(To Goren.)* He won't win anything. I'll see to that!

But Kovacs quickly established that he would donate any winnings to the Save The Children Foundation, and Groucho played it straight. The quiz rules that season were another variation on the four-in-a-row right, you win, two-in-a-row wrong, you're out formula. Now, the four-in-a-row correct entitled them to spin the wheel at the end of the show

Groucho with bridge expert Charles Goren, a contestant on *You Bet Your Life* (radio play date March 31, 1958 and television air date April 3, 1958). (Courtesy Paul Wesolowski)

As Long As They're Laughing

for a prize that could be $2,000 or, if the right number came up, $10,000. The big-money shows had pushed us that far. If they missed one of the preliminary questions, they lost half of what they had accumulated so far. However, to further complicate the situation, they had the option of keeping what they had won to that point and not risking it on the wheel. It took George some time, that season, to explain the rules.

Adding a bit of spice to the occasion was the presence, as Mr. Kovacs' partner, of Miss Sanita Pelkey, an extremely shapely 21-year-old chorus girl from the Moulin Rouge night club.

Groucho explained the rules to Sanita and Mr. Kovacs. "If you get four in a row right," he said, "it'll be a miracle!"

But Miss Pelkey had selected "Mother Goose Rhymes" as their category, and, to Ernie's delighted surprise, she knew some of the answers. She knew that you "went around the Mulberry bush early in the morning" and that "Little Jack Horner pulled a plum out of his Christmas pie." But she came up blank when Groucho asked, "Who went to sea, silver buckles at his knee?"

"That's a darned good question," Kovacs said, turning to the audience. "Anybody out there know the answer? What's the one with the pussycat and the boots and all that jazz?"

"No," Groucho said, "that comes much later."

The bell rang. "It's Bobby Shaftoe."

"Who?" asked Kovacs.

"I think he's an agent, handles some big stars," Groucho explained.

So they had one wrong. But the girl knew the next two, that in the rhyme "one, two, buckle my shoe," nine, ten rhymes with big fat hen, and that "some like it in the pot nine days old."

The next question asked, "Why did pussycat go to London?"

"Is this any particular pussycat?" Kovacs wanted to know and then came up with the answer, "To see the Queen! Is that right?" he asked. "If it's not right, I retract it!"

Fenneman said, "That's right."

They now had three in a row right.

"Who saw cock robin die?" Groucho asked.

"Let's be careful. Let's not rush into this," Ernie said. "Does it have wings and six legs?"

"No," Groucho said, "I know that one. That's a garbage wagon."

"I'm going to see if he has anything in his face when I do little hints." Ernie made buzzing sounds like a fly. "He smiled, but he's tricky."

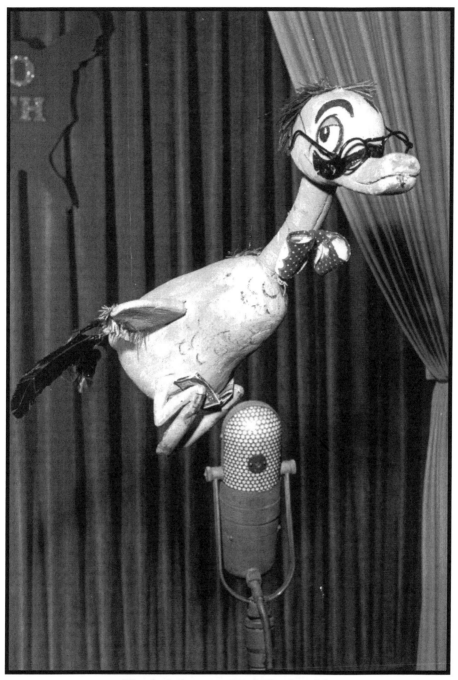

The duck (courtesy Paul Wesolowski)

" 'I,' said the fly, 'with my little eye'," the girl declared.

"The fly is right!" Groucho shouted. "You got four in a row and win a thousand dollars!"

Ernie, having heard Mr. Goren say the secret word, immediately started shouting, "Name! Name!" and gesturing toward the loft where the duck was nesting. "Name! Name!"

After he had said the word six times, and it was obvious he was not going to give up the gag, I signaled to the orchestra, the trumpet sounded, "Stars and Stripes" was played, and the duck dropped into view.

"It's dishonest," Groucho said, "but since this is counterfeit money, we don't care. Here's 50 for you and 50 for you."

Kovacs looked at the money. "Who's this President, Jim Clinton?"

"He made coats for the Army and Navy," Groucho said. And, on the fake stage money the duck carried, the President's name was, indeed, Clinton. Incidentally, they decided not to risk half of their $1,000 on a possible $10,000 because, as Ernie said, "It's the Children's Fund kids' money."

The original still reads: An attentive Groucho Marx gets an earful of advice from his six-and-one-half-year-old daughter Melinda following a recent *You Bet Your Life* comedy-quiz show. The young lass, who appeared recently on the NBC radio-TV show, will be a guest again soon...and again, and again... 2/20/53 (Photofest)

As Long As They're Laughing

CHAPTER 8
Tell Me a Story, Sing Me a Song

Groucho Marx was not a stand-up comic even though some of his fame did rest on remarks that came close to being one-liners. I once asked him for his favorite line. "Stonewalls do not a Jackson make," he replied. It would be my choice, too. For semantic anarchy, it has few peers, and in its efficiency, it has the quality mathematicians call "elegance."

Two other brief lines are also high on my list, both of them in the equine sub-category. "I'd horsewhip you, if I had a horse," from *Horse Feathers,* is a remark I cherish and frequently quote whether it is strictly pertinent or not. The other "horse" line is "...going like a horse-afire," applied indiscriminately to any rapid sequence of events or actions. It has the added virtue of making some kind of sense.

Max Eastman's 1936 book *The Enjoyment of Laughter* [1] is a book I have always admired as one of the best theoretical analyses of comedy. He devotes some time to a consideration of the "horsewhip" line, concluding that it is not technically a joke, but merely a funny saying, because it has no point. He contrasts it to another passage from *Cocoanuts* in which Groucho said, "Three years ago I came to Florida without a nickel in my pocket. Now I have a nickel in my pocket." That, Eastman says, is a joke because it does have a point.

To give him his due, Eastman based his theory of comedy on two elements, surprise and playfulness, epitomized in the image of a crawling child who laughs when a toy is playfully snatched away from him. In the "horsewhip" line, we are promised a meaning, but it is snatched away. The promised meaning is replaced, not by another meaning, but by nonsense. It is, therefore, not a joke. The "nickel" bit, however, replaces the expected meaning with another, surprising, meaning, and is, therefore, a joke. This does not explain why the "horsewhip" line is funnier than the "nickel" joke. Groucho had no patience with such hair splitting, of course. He did not think jokes should be explained. On those occasions when I did question the rational basis for a line of dialogue or a piece of

"What do you care, as long as they're laughing?" (Courtesy Paul Wesolowski)

business, his most likely response was, "What do you care, as long as they're laughing?" The source of that defiant dictum, he told me, was

The Klein Brothers, a Vaudeville act of the early 1900s, with a routine in which the comic delivered a dramatic speech consisting of pure gibberish. The audience always laughed. The straight man then said, "What was that all about?"

The comic replied, "What do you care as long as they're laughing?"

Groucho also enjoyed telling a select number of conventionally constructed jokes, sometimes in conversation, most often in public appearances, and especially in the regular session before a *You Bet Your Life* performance.

One story he especially liked was firmly based in reality, but was also a rare exception to two of his self-imposed rules. When his daughter Melinda was six years old and had just started to school, he introduced this anecdote into the pre-show routine.

> My daughter Melinda goes to kindergarten now, and the other day I asked her what she did in school. She said, "All we do is paint and go to the toilet." (Pronounced almost, but not quite, "terlet.")

He never told that joke on the air. One of his earliest dictums was, "No terlet jokes." The second thing that made it exceptional was that it was almost the only time that he used a personal reference in his comedy. On *You Bet Your Life,* he relied substantially on free association and the rapid combing of his memory and subconscious for references and cross-references. Yet, in all those hundreds of programs, I can remember very few allusions to his family or his private life. There were, during that period, many times of turmoil and emotional strain. The breakup of his marriage, his divorce and subsequent remarriage, his worries about his daughter Miriam's health, and many complicated dealings with networks, movie studios, and the tax department—none of this ever surfaced in performance. He did occasionally speak of his son Arthur and his prowess as a championship tennis player, and one time when we had a department store Santa Claus as a guest, we got a fleeting glimpse of family relations in the Marx household.

"I remember when my kid was around 12 years old," Groucho said. "That's Arthur, he's 26 now and works at MGM. He wanted to get one of those air rifles. He kept insisting, and I said, 'No, no. I don't want you to have an air rifle.' But he kept insisting, and finally I said, 'Look, as long as I'm head of the house, you're not going to have a gun!' And he said, 'If I get a gun, you won't be the head of the house!'"

Occasionally, something one of our guests said triggered a memory of his early life, and, over the years, some corners of his youth and the days on the road were briefly illuminated. Once, we got a glimpse of the early days of their Vaudeville career. Groucho was talking to a young boy named Ben Zeppa. Groucho asked, "How old are you, Ben?" Ben replied, "I'm 13." Groucho reminisced:

> I never was 13. I was 12 once. In fact, I was 12 for about eight years. All the brothers were. We used to travel in Vaudeville. If you were 12 or under, you could travel for half fare on the train. My mother used to travel with us then. We didn't need her, but she thought we did. When the conductor asked her for the tickets, she gave him four half-fare tickets. He said, "Where are the kids?" and she said, "They're around the train someplace." He looked in the washroom, and my brother Harpo was shaving — this is true — the other two boys were in the baggage car shooting dice, and I was making a play for a dame across the aisle. The conductor came back and said, "Mrs. Marx, if those kids are under 12, I'm too young to be running this train," and he jumped off at the next station.

Another guest was named Araxi Jamogchian.

"What should I call you? Araxi?" Groucho asked.

"Everyone calls me Roxie," she said.

"No, no, anything but that!" Groucho said. "I played the Roxy. We had five performances a day and six on Saturdays and Sundays. If you must have a nickname, I'll call you Palace or The Majestic Theatre in Chicago."

Groucho takes a coffee break outside his dressing room. (Courtesy Paul Wesolowski)

In December 1956 we taped a show which aired in February 1957, in which our special guest was Mr. David Ewen, distinguished musicologist, author of some 35 books, including several standard reference works. He was there to plug his new biography of Richard Rogers. Groucho asked him the usual question about how he met his wife.

"We were just friends," Mr. Ewen said, "and one day I happened to tell her that I played poker with the Marx Brothers. She was as crazy about the Marx Brothers as I was, so that was the day love walked in."

"You couldn't have played poker with the Marx Brothers," Groucho said. "None of us ever had any money."

"But I did," Ewen said.

"You sound pretty bitter," Groucho said. "You'd better tell us the whole story."

"You were appearing on the Broadway musical stage for the first time. I think it was *I'll Say She Is,* " Ewen replied.

"Were you married then?" Groucho asked.

"No," Ewen said. "I was a youngster. 1925. I was born in 1907, so I was 18."

"What went on during the game?" Groucho asked.

"I came down to interview you for one of the magazines," Ewen replied. "When I came in you were in full costume already, and there were five of you, because there were five brothers then, and you were playing poker. What I didn't know was that playing poker with the Marx Brothers was not an orthodox procedure. I was asking you questions, and, while you were making me punch drunk with your crazy answers, Chico would look into my cards, he would signal Harpo, and then, when Harpo had better cards than I had, he would raise me. When he had worse cards, he would tear up his cards, and Chico would give him another five cards. When the game was over, I didn't have an interview, and I didn't have any money because I lost seven bucks."

"That sounds like the Marx Brothers all right," Groucho said. "What happened? Did you call the cops?"

"No, I didn't," Ewen said. "Chico gave me back the seven bucks."

"Then it couldn't have been the Marx Brothers," Groucho said. "Must have been the Dolly Sisters."

On other aspects of his private life, he never tried to evade the obvious fact that he was Jewish, but he never exploited a Jewish constituency. He did not approve of those Jewish comedians who got easy laughs by using Yiddish words that were old familiars to the Jewish contingent and sounded vaguely dirty to the Gentiles. He told a few religious jokes, this one with fair success in the pre-show warm-up for *You Bet Your Life.*

> A Catholic girl was in love with a Jewish
> boy, and her mother suggested that she try
> to convert him. After about six weeks, the
> mother asked for a progress report. "I think
> I'm doing too well," the girl said. "Now
> he wants to become a priest!"

There was another that he occasionally used that I think he considered a Catholic joke.

> The Wise Men came to see the infant Jesus,
> and they enthused over his beauty. But his
> mother, Mary, was disconsolate. "What's
> the matter?" they asked. "I did so want a
> girl," she said.

That was usually balanced by the one purely Jewish anecdote I can remember his telling.

> Otto Kahn, the banker, didn't like the idea
> that he was a Jew. He was walking down
> 5th Avenue with Marshall B. Wilder, who
> had a hunched back. As they walked, they
> passed a synagogue. Kahn turned to Wilder
> and said, "You know, I used to be a Jew."
> And Wilder said, "Yes, I know, I used to
> be a hunchback."

One of his other religious stories combined the two faiths. He used it regularly when we toured with his play *Time For Elizabeth*. After the third act curtain, Groucho appeared with what was always the most successful part of the evening, about 20 minutes of carefully crafted stories and observations.

> A rabbi and a priest are seated opposite
> each other in a railroad dining car. The
> priest orders ham and eggs. "Did you ever

A Clean Sweep . . . "YOU BET YOUR LIFE

Thanks to 500 U. S. and Canada Radio-TV Editors in Motion
Picture Daily's Annual Poll for Fame Magazine

BEST AUDIENCE PARTICIPATION SHOW ....RADIO
BEST QUIZ SHOW ....RADIO
BEST QUIZ SHOW ....TV
ONE OF CHAMPIONS OF ALL RADIO SHOWS

GROUCHO MARX.........................{ ....ONE OF BEST COMEDIANS
                                    { ONE OF BEST MASTER OF CEREMONIES*

Thanks from GROUCHO and Producer JOHN GUEDEL
Thanks to Co-Directors Bob Dwan and Bernie Smith
and all the rest of the boys who deserve to call these awards their own

*P. S. By the way, Groucho also won the Emmy for Outstanding TV Personality of 1950

The first year *You Bet Your Life* aired on television, the show was voted best quiz show and Groucho won the Emmy for Outstanding Television Personality of 1950.

> try ham?" he asks the rabbi. "You ought to
> try it. You'll like it." "Did you ever go out
> with a girl?" the rabbi asks. "You ought to
> try it. It's even better than ham."

"...go out with a girl?" is exactly the wording Groucho used when he told the story to a theatre audience. It worked just as well as any of the more explicit terms that might be used today (and that he used in private conversation).

He told one story which, because of its nature, never got a big laugh, but it had a special resonance for him. He told it one night on *You Bet Your Life* to Norman Carroll, a charming man who had once been a clown and was at that time ringmaster for the Ringling Brothers, Barnum & Bailey Circus.

> A man went to a doctor in Paris. He was
> terribly depressed, wanted to kill himself.
> "The best medicine I know is laughter,"
> the doctor said. "My prescription for you
> is that you go to the circus tonight and see
> Grock the clown." The man said, "I am
> Grock the clown."

I think he especially enjoyed a story he often told that harked back to Vaudeville days.

> A small-time Vaudevillian was staying in a family-run boarding house in a mid-Western town. At the first meal, all the guests were seated at a long table, and the actor, who, of course, was late, found a seat at the end. The father of the family stood up at the head of the table and began to say grace. "Louder," the actor called out. "I can't hear you." The man looked up and said, "I wasn't speaking to you."

He had one Irish joke that I liked.

> There was a wake, and Paddy O'Neal was laid out in his coffin in the parlor. Some of the neighbors came over to pay their respects. "My, my," they said. "You can hardly believe he's dead. He still looks warm." Mrs. O'Neal said, "Hot or cold, he goes out in the morning."

Most of his repertoire, however, was based on actuality. He loved to tell of the time when there was a baseball game between the Vaudevillians who were appearing on rival circuits in Baltimore. Groucho hit a grounder which was thrown to Will Rogers who was playing second base. "You're out!" Rogers said. "But you're not anywhere near second base," Groucho protested. "Son," Rogers said, "when you get to be my age, wherever you're standing is second base."

The last time I was in Rome, I made a pilgrimage to the spot on which the event occurred that was the basis for his most consistently successful story. He used it often in the pre-program routine for *You Bet Your Life,* consistently in the *Time For Elizabeth* curtain speech, and, finally, in his triumphant Carnegie Hall Concert in 1972. I can recite it by heart.

> I was staying at the Hassler Hotel in Rome.
> I had just stepped away from the entrance

The American Broadcasting Company
takes great pride in congratulating

GROUCHO MARX

His Partner and Producer, JOHN GUEDEL, and Members of the Staff of

"YOU BET YOUR LIFE"

Bob Dwan, Bernie Smith, Hy Friedman, Ed Tyler, Eddie Mills,
Dorothy Nye, George Fenneman, Jerry Fielding, George Otte

Cited By

THE GEORGE FOSTER PEABODY AWARDS COMMITTEE

for the "best entertainment in COMEDY"

◆

Other ABC citations by this year's Peabody Awards Committee:

COMMUNISM—U. S. BRAND, ABC's documentary broadcast, radio's "outstanding educational program."
ACTOR'S STUDIO. ABC's dramatic video series—"outstanding contribution to the art of television for
its uninhibited and brilliant pioneering in the field of televised drama."

ABC American Broadcasting Company

The Network That Brought You Transcribed Programs First

and stopped to light a very expensive cigar.
Someone bumped me from behind, and I
dropped the cigar in the gutter. "Christ,"
I said, then looked up and saw a Catholic
priest standing beside me. I was embarrassed. Here I was, a stranger in the Holy
City, and I had just committed blasphemy.

I was about to apologize, when the priest
reached within the folds of his garment and
drew out a cigar. "Mr. Marx," he said, "I
believe you just said the secret word!"

It is my recollection that most of the time he told the story, he respected
what he felt were Catholic sensibilities and used the word "hell" instead
of "Christ." I am absolutely certain I am accurate in quoting the phrase,
"the priest reached within the folds of his garment...." He always used
exactly those words, probably because he liked the sound of them, and
I have always liked them because their rhythm, precision, and faintly
archaic air embody some of the notable aspects of Groucho's personal
style.

Another story based on an actual happening emerged one evening
in the course of a *You Bet Your Life* performance. He was speaking to
the famous trial lawyer, Louis Nizer, and somehow the subject of *Time*
magazine and publisher Henry Luce came up.

Speaking of Luce, I've got to tell you a
story. I was at a dinner party one night,
out in Bel Air someplace, and my dinner
partner was Claire Booth Luce. She was
ambassador to the Vatican at the time. She
didn't have a car, she came there in a cab.
Around midnight the party broke up, and
somebody suggested that I take Mrs. Luce
home. So she got in the car with me—it
was one of those foggy nights in Bel Air,
and I couldn't find the place where she was
living. I finally got out of the car—there
was a lamp post there, and she got out, and
I started to climb the lamp post. There are
big clumps of bushes around each lamp
post in Bel Air. I'm climbing up there,
looking for the name of the street, and just
then Charlie Brackett, the writer, comes
along. He walks his dog every night at
midnight. He looks over and says, "Well
I've seen everything, but I never thought

I'd see Groucho Marx and the Ambassador
to the Vatican in the bushes in Bel Air!'"

Groucho also loved to sing. His first public appearance was as a singer. At the age of five, he made his debut at the Old Homestead Beer Garden on New York's East Side. His first regular paying job was for a dollar a week in the boys' choir at the Episcopal Church on Madison Avenue. He remembered earning a dollar for singing while perched on a barrel in Coney Island. At 14, he entered Vaudeville as a boy singer with the Leroy Trio, a job which ended when he was stranded in Cripple Creek, Colorado. He was back on the road again, still singing, six months later in an act called *Lily Seville and Master Marx.* That tour lasted until Fort Worth, Texas, where Lily ran off with the animal trainer on the bill. She also absconded with the boy's emergency supply of money, hidden in what all Vaudevillians called a grouch bag, a leather pouch usually worn around the neck. It is a matter of controversy whether that term was the source of Mr. Marx's later famous name.

His career as a singer continued, however. At age 15, a year before his mother Minnie organized *The Three Nightingales,* young Julius joined the famous Gus Edwards troupe in an act called, that season, *Postal Telegraph Boys.* He sang "Farewell Killarney" and even had his picture on the sheet music when it was published. One month after joining Edwards, the company took part in a huge benefit for "the sufferers of the San Francisco earthquake." Forty-five years later on *You Bet Your Life,* Groucho remembered the occasion when he appeared on the stage of the Metropolitan Opera House on the same bill with Enrico Caruso and John McCormack and sang his song, "Somebody's Sweetheart I Want to Be." "Everyone was in full dress," he said. "Up until then, I had never seen anyone in full dress, except my father when he got married."

Over the years, Groucho acquired an affection for the songs of Gilbert and Sullivan, and one of his chief pleasures was to sit at home and sing the patter songs, accompanying himself on his guitar. His appearance in the television production of *The Mikado* in 1960 was the fulfillment of a long-held dream, but the occasion was not without its difficulties. The producers of *The Bell Telephone Hour* did everything in their power to meet his conditions and even some fairly unreasonable demands, including having his daughter Melinda, then age 14, cast as one of the "three little maids from school," and having his wife, Eden, appear in the cho-

Groucho and Martyn Green discuss *The Bell Telephone Hour* production of *The Mikado*. (Courtesy Paul Wesolowski)

rus. But they spared no expense on the rest of the cast, lining up a truly luminous roster. Helen Traubel was Katisha, Stanley Holloway, Poo Bah, and Dennis King the Mikado. From the Metropolitan Opera came Robert Rounseville to play the wandering minstrel and Barbara Meister as Yum Yum.

Martyn Green, the great Gilbert and Sullivan star, was one of the producers on the project. Green's specialty had been the very kind of comedy roles of which Ko-Ko, the hapless Lord High Executioner, was a prime example. He was one of the great patter-song singers and especially excelled at some intricate eccentric dances which had become his trademark. But all that was over. About a year before, he had been in a strange accident in an automatic parking garage. Somehow his left leg had become lodged beneath the huge automobile elevator and was, finally, amputated.

ONE MAN ON A CHAIR

Has Drawn More Viewers
Over the Last Six Years
Than Any Other Attraction
On Television.

When Green arrived in Hollywood several weeks before the production, he was in good, if somewhat subdued, spirits. He was affable, co-operative, and entirely reasonable in his demands. It was my job as associate producer to work with him in preparing the one-hour adaptation of the script. (Fifty-two minutes, really, allowing for commercials, titles, and credits.) I had made a preliminary cut, working from a set of Green's recording of *The Mikado*, and he accepted my version almost without change.

The difficulty was subtle and psychological. Groucho had to be aware of Green on the set, in a wheelchair, unable to perform, unable even to demonstrate any of the moves. It had to be inhibiting. To make matters worse, they had designed a costume for Groucho as Ko-Ko, featuring some large sail-like appendages on the trousers, making it almost impossible for him to move. And finally, the rigidity of the time constraints, squeezing the whole thing into 52 minutes, left no room for improvisation, not even the occasional antic move. The result was a quite respectable, straightforward performance, but without much of the extra dimension everyone was hoping Groucho would bring to the role. Working with Helen Traubel was a real pleasure — it was worth the price of admission to hear her sing "May Not a Cheated Maiden Die?" and Stanley Holloway was a delight onstage and off. In spite of all the problems, the broadcast received the highest rating the series had won all season and, particularly satisfying, the second half of the program got a bigger rating than the opening. The recording, which was a separate session, came out very well. Goddard Lieberson, head of Columbia Recording and an old friend of Groucho's, came out from New York to produce the session. Most of the strain had disappeared, and the album holds up splendidly today.

Nevertheless, the rehearsals for the television show were a great strain, and Groucho felt it. During a lunch break for one of the sessions, we went to a restaurant across the street from the NBC studios in Burbank. Groucho glanced at the menu and then said to the waitress, "Bring me some hemlock." The waitress left and returned in a few minutes.

"I'm sorry, sir," she said. "We're all out of hemlock."

For one of the few times in his career, Groucho was speechless.

(Photofest)

CHAPTER 9
The Marxian Mind

During a break in rehearsal for *The Mikado*, Groucho was in conversation with Martyn Green. Groucho was speaking of his pleasure in the company of Peter Ustinov.

"Yes," Green said, "he's a delightful companion if you can get him to talk sense, which he does brilliantly, but only for a few moments."

"I think he thinks making sense doesn't make sense," Groucho said.

One brief interlude in *You Bet Your Life* stays in my mind because of its beautiful irrationality. One evening around 1955, there was a lull in the proceedings. George was waiting to be asked, "Who's next?" Groucho, for no reason, started to sing, to the tune of "Lydia The Tattooed Lady."

> Edward Stettinius,
> Oh Edward Stettinius,
> Stettinius....*(He trailed off.)*
> All right, George, who's next?
> (For the record, Stettinius was Secretary
> of State in 1945.)

On vacation in Europe, we were in Amsterdam on a sight-seeing boat, puttering slowly through the lovely canals. A guide with a megaphone was doing nothing to add to the natural charm with his drone of statistics. Eventually, he asked for questions. Groucho raised his hand. "Can you tell me the latest Neilson on the *Pinky Lee Show*?"

Through the long years of traveling in Vaudeville, a good deal of his struggle against organized stupidity had taken place in restaurants. Groucho knew in advance that he would be placed under the air-conditioning vent, next to the clattering service tray, and in a direct line with the loud speaker. The rye bread would be stale, the potato salad made with mayonnaise, and the lamb chops overdone. In Chicago, he studied the menu glumly for a long 10 minutes. "Bring me Thousand Island dressing and coffee," he said.

He tried to get some butter in a small cafe in Hamburg, Germany. After three unsuccessful attempts, he summoned the waiter one more time. "If we can't have butter, bring us some guns."

When I began to work with Groucho, I first had to learn how to talk to him. It was a skill that took considerable nerve, and a knowledge of how his mind worked. The challenge arose because, especially in the beginning, he rarely let a complete sentence pass without an interruption:

DWAN:	*(On the telephone.)* Groucho....
GROUCHO:	Oh, it's you again.
DWAN:	Yes. Groucho, I....
GROUCHO:	You just said that.
DWAN:	It's about the show tonight. We have a peculiar...
GROUCHO:	All our shows are peculiar.
DWAN:	...problem with one of our contestants....
GROUCHO:	All our *contestants* are peculiar.
DWAN:	The problem is that this one is 93 years old.
GROUCHO:	That's *his* problem. Serves him right for leading such a dull life.
DWAN:	Anyway, he's from Hawaii....
GROUCHO:	From where?
DWAN:	Hawaii.
GROUCHO:	I'm all right, how are you?

It made no difference how I said it, he reacted as every Vaudevillian would to the standard early 20th century pronunciation, "Huh-wy-uh."

I soon learned to accept the interruptions and proceed as if it were a normal conversation.

In such interchanges, Groucho was driven partly by a conscious interest in testing me to learn whether I could perform under fire. As years went by, happily, he evidently felt less need to conduct the ordeal by word, and our dialogue became less jagged. In large part, of course, his responses were semi-automatic, driven by a compulsion to make the play on words, to reverse the logic.

Ralph Levy, George Fenneman and Groucho and I discuss *You Bet Your Life.* **Ralph, a very good director, directed a pilot for CBS. (Courtesy Paul Wesolowski)**

His reply to "Hawaii" was a reflex, as it was to a short list of other words. Bernie Smith went to extreme lengths to contrive situations in which contestants would say one of the trigger words. If we had a banker on the show, he would be sure to be asked, "Where do you have to go when the bank runs out of money?" The proper response was, "Down to the vaults," and Groucho would keep after him until he produced the right word.

"To where?"

"The vaults."

"Valtz? I'd be glad to. Would you care to lead?"

He got someone once to talk about a dense forest. It took some doing, but the forest ranger or lumberjack was led into repeating the word "dense" so that Groucho could say, "Dense? I'd love to! Would you prefer the rumba or the cha-cha-cha?"

Anyone in the Army might be asked, "What has replaced the horses in the cavalry?" to which he would be expected to reply, "Tanks," and Groucho would answer, "You're welcome!" (Or a wine grower would be asked, "Where do you store your bulk wine?" to which "barrels" was not an acceptable answer.)

He created his own private geography of place names during the course of *You Bet Your Life* conversations.

He was speaking to a young married couple, Doctors Lloyd and Ann Ely, who had met while students in medical school. She said that their first meeting was while they were working on "adjacent cadavers."

GROUCHO: What a lovely name for a summer resort. "Spending a weekend at Adjacent Cadavers. Wish you were here."

As the conversation continued, she said that she didn't like Lloyd at first because she resented the way he asked her for a date to a dance.

DOCTOR: I thought it sounded like I was a last resort.
GROUCHO: Here we are, back at Adjacent Cadavers!

Another of his creations occurred when he was questioning some parents about how they disciplined their children. The mother said she occasionally had to "whack 'em on the bum bum."

GROUCHO: Oh, I know it well. It's a resort in the North of England. "Where are you going this summer?" "Thought we'd toddle up to Whack'em on the Bum Bum!"

On December 5, 1945, he wrote to Sam Zolotow of the *New York Times* drama department.

> My plans are still in embryo. In case you've never been there, this is a small town on the outskirts of wishful thinking.[1]

Groucho and film cowboy star Hoot Gibson on the show in January, 1956 (Photofest)

A companion conceit appears in a letter he wrote to his daughter Miriam on December 20, 1945, apparently in response to an early Christmas gift.

> I received the Steig cartoon book this
> morning and read it with avidity. (Avid-

ity is an Armenian neighbor of mine who
lives across the street and he always drops
over whenever I have a book of Steig's
cartoons.)[2]

Little glimpses of how his mind worked frequently appeared without
warning. We were walking down the street in Beverly Hills when he
suddenly said:

The greatest man who ever lived was the
man who invented sitting down.

We were having lunch with Harry Ruby at Nate and Al's Delicates-
sen in Beverly Hills when he explained to me the difference between the
waiters on the West Coast and those in New York at Lindy's.

They're not as sharp here. Here, they're on
film. In New York, they're live.

Another of his notable inventions took place in a Beverly Hills
restaurant, this one involving no words at all. As was our custom, we
were having dinner at Chasen's after a performance. There was a large
party in an alcove just behind us, celebrating a birthday. When a waiter
approached bearing a large cake with burning candles, Groucho got up,
took the cake and brought it to the table. He had the guest of honor blow
out the candles, and then, with the help of the waiter, served a piece of
the cake to everyone in the party. Everyone accepted the service and no
one recognized the server. He was delighted.

We had a more extensive sample of the Marxian mind at work, un-
shackled by any script, in a break between contestants during a performance of *You Bet Your Life.*

FENNEMAN: (*after the first couple had made its exit):* Before we
          go on, may I make an announcement?
GROUCHO: Well, you may. I don't approve of it, but you may.
FENNEMAN: This is an announcement for a doctor in our audi-
          ence — there's nothing wrong with anybody here at
          the show...

GROUCHO:	The hell there isn't.
FENNEMAN:	Dr. Hoyt, one of the pages...
GROUCHO:	Dr. Hoyt! That's a fine name for a doctor! Dr. Hoyt!
FENNEMAN:	Dr. Hoyt, one of the pages has a call for you, sir...
GROUCHO:	It's probably Clotworthy having another kid.
	(Bill Clotworthy represented the advertising agency, BBDO, on the show.)
GROUCHO:	Doctor, why don't you pay your bills so they won't be badgering you in the middle of a performance? You know, that was an old joke of Bob Benchley's years ago. It happened in a theatre up in Boston, on the opening night of a very important play. Benchley was kind of lit, and he stood up in the middle of the first act, during a very dramatic scene, and said, "Is there a doctor in the house?" A doctor stood up in the balcony and said, "I'm a doctor." And Benchley said, "How do you like the show, Doc?"

In 1972, in one of his last public appearances, Groucho did a one-man concert at Carnegie Hall. One of his bits was an anecdote and song I had never heard him do before. But it is a perfect example of what he would create as comedy when left entirely to his own resources.

When we did *Animal Crackers,* we needed
two minutes for a change, so I wrote... the
most ridiculous poem you could possibly
write and tried it on the audience. The first
10 weeks we did the show, we used to get
a sophisticated New York audience, and
they used to laugh and applaud at the end.
Then you started getting the out-of-town
crowd, and they thought it was serious.
Here's the way it goes:

Did you ever sit and ponder as you walk
along the Strand
That life's a bitter battle at the best,
And if you only knew it and would lend a
helping hand,

Universal
presents

"ANIMAL CRACKERS"
Starring
THE 4 MARX BROS.
GROUCHO, HARPO, CHICO, ZEPPO
with
LILLIAN ROTH
and
MARGARET DUMONT, LOUIS SORIN, HAL THOMPSON
MARGARET IRVING, KATHRYN REECE, ROBERT GREIG, EDWARD METCALF

Directed by VICTOR HEERMAN   Screenplay by MORRIE RYSKIND

Based on the Musical Play by
GEORGE S. KAUFMAN, MORRIE RYSKIND,
BERT KALMAR, HARRY RUBY

A UNIVERSAL RELEASE G GENERAL AUDIENCES

THE CAST

Captain Jeffrey Spaulding	GROUCHO MARX
The Professor	HARPO MARX
Signor Emanuel Ravelli	CHICO MARX
Horatio Jamison	ZEPPO MARX
Arabella Rittenhouse	LILLIAN ROTH
Mrs. Rittenhouse	MARGARET DUMONT
Roscoe Chandler	LOUIS SORIN
John Parker	HAL THOMPSON
Mrs. Whitehead	MARGARET IRVING
Grace Carpenter	KATHRYN REECE
Hives	ROBERT GREIG
Hennessey	EDWARD METCALF
Six Footmen	THE MUSIC MASTERS

THE CREDITS

Directed by	VICTOR HEERMAN
Screenplay by	MORRIE RYSKIND

Based on the Musical Play by
GEORGE S. KAUFMAN, MORRIE RYSKIND, BERT KALMAR, HARRY RUBY

Photographed by	GEORGE FOLSEY
Continuity	PIERRE COLLINGS

Then every man could meet the final
test.
The world is but a stage, my friend,
And life is but a game,
And how you play is all that
Matters in the end,

For whether a man is right or wrong,
A woman gets the blame,
And your mother is your dog's best
friend.
Then up came mighty Casey
and strode up to the bat,
And Sheridan was 50 miles away.
For it takes a heap of lovin',
to make a home like that,
On the road to where the flyin' fishes
play.

Then I used to take a chair, which Vaudeville actors used to do in those days, and I
would start walking off the stage, and the
last line would be:

Be a real live Pagliacci and *(sung)* laugh,
clown, laugh![3]

There exists, fortuitously, a recording of Groucho in a circumstance in which he was certifiably without script or preparation. By a second fortunate circumstance, he is paired with his good friend, Fred Allen, another artist devoted to words and antic ideas. Groucho thought highly of Fred, considering him to be the brightest and wittiest of his peers.

Early in the summer of 1953, Fred Allen produced the first program in his television series, *Judge For Yourself*, on a Hollywood sound stage, which happened to be in the rear of the same building where we had the *You Bet Your Life* editing rooms. Groucho had been alerted to the occasion by friendly spies, and, after the performance, he walked into the studio, unannounced, without any warning to Fred. Here, recorded for me by an accommodating engineer, are the two master ad libbers faced with the challenge of starting from scratch. Not great comedy, perhaps, but a glimpse of a couple of old pros indulging in what Max Eastman called "the enjoyment of laughter."

(After the initial greetings, Fred explains to his audience.)

FRED: Mr. Marx has detected some flaws in our show, and is going to do the whole program over.

(Groucho starts by using what is at hand, the audience, a stage prop, the physical studio. It is an old-fashioned sound stage with huge loading doors and sound locks. He applies the reliable technique of slight exaggeration.)

GROUCHO: The nice thing about this place, nobody can escape while the show is on.
FRED: Yes. They also remove the air.

(After a few minutes of sparring, they start to use the audience.)

GROUCHO: Are these people going to be here every week?
FRED: These people are glued to the seats. I think they're a better class than you get at your show.
GROUCHO: I don't know if they're any better—it's the same crowd—just a little older, that's all.

(Then he notices a huge prop can of Campbell's Soup—Fred's sponsor.)

GROUCHO: I don't know how they get everybody in that Campbell can.
FRED: Campbell's in there, himself, most of the time.
GROUCHO: He's either making soup or burying people in New York.

(Only Fred and a few people in the audience get the reference to Campbell's mortuary in New York.)

GROUCHO: I think it's a wonderful audience, and I think it's really a great show. You may wind up with a sponsor like DeSoto.
FRED: Oh, I don't think so....
GROUCHO: Is there an ashtray in the audience?
FRED: Is there a writer in the audience? Well, I think this is not bad, for no material.

Two of the many famous visitors to _You Bet Your Life_: Gummo and Groucho with Deborah Kerr and Edward G. Robinson. (Courtesy Paul Wesolowski)

GROUCHO: Well, don't get an automobile for a sponsor... then you'll have to buy one of those cars, too. In the old days, I was on for Elgin compacts. All I had to do is buy a $3 compact. You wouldn't want to give a girl an automobile, would you?

FRED: I worked for Sal Hepatica for eight years.

GROUCHO: Well, there's nothing like starting from the bottom.

FRED: I think that now we have gotten one collective laugh, that was yours, I think we should....

GROUCHO: It was your feed-line, Fred. If you hadn't taken that Sal Hepatica, I never would have had the answer.

FRED: I never would have had the problems I had.

GROUCHO: I predict, if we stand here for five more minutes, the place will be raided.

FRED: I think if we stand here 10 minutes, Vaudeville will come back.

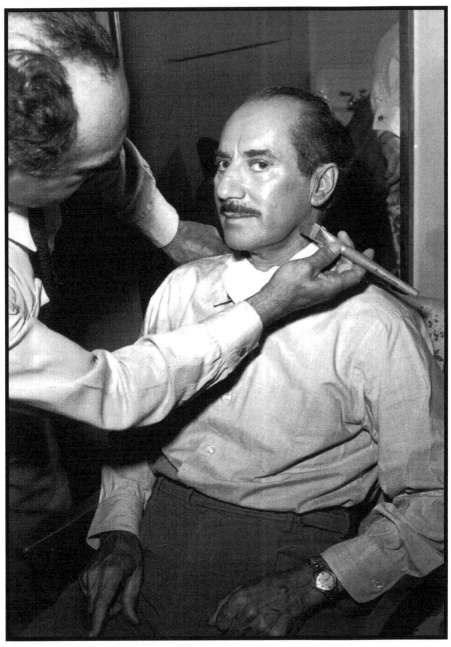

Groucho in the makeup chair before a *You Bet Your Life* performance. (Photofest)

GROUCHO: Whatever happened to Vaudeville, Fred? I'll give you a straight line like George Burns. I should be leaning against the side. I'll lean against you, Fred.

FRED:	Vaudeville... I don't know... someone said... Bob Hope said that Vaudeville died, and television is the box it came back in.
GROUCHO:	You had some very attractive girls on your show tonight, Fred. Do you mind if I use them in August?
FRED:	No, I think they'll still be attractive in this climate. Most of ours are decomposed.
GROUCHO:	We've used up all the contestants out here. We're planning on Forest Lawn for the fall.
FRED:	Well, with the climate... I understand they have a man at Forest Lawn who goes around every day with a shovel and hits the ground so the people don't grow again. A woman named Lily came half way up out there the other day. Well, I want to thank Groucho for coming down here to help me launch this thing without the champagne.
GROUCHO:	That comes later.
FRED:	Later?
GROUCHO:	First we have to get the launch.
FRED:	Well, I go out to launch every day.
GROUCHO:	Shall we leave?
FRED:	Yes, we shall leave.
GROUCHO:	Come, Mr. Gallagher....

(They exit.)

Penultimately, I must record for posterity one of his favorite dictums:

Always be glad you're not at the dentist.

And finally, I remember vividly his most effective rejoinder when I complained about any difficulty in the production of our show.

Nobody told you you *had* to go into show business.

George Fenneman and Groucho (Photofest)

As Long As They're Laughing

CHAPTER 10
Fenneman

On an evening in 1950, George Fenneman introduced the second pair of contestants on an episode of *You Bet Your Life*.

> We have a couple of single girls who are anxious to talk to you, Groucho. Dolores Olson and Sandy Silence, will you come in please and meet Groucho Marx.

Two attractive young women entered. Groucho greeted them with his customary:

> Welcome to *You Bet Your Life*. Say the secret word and divide a hundred dollars. It's a common word, something you find around the house.

Fenneman, meanwhile, adjusted their microphones to the proper height for their close-up camera and made his exit to his listening post offstage. Groucho consulted the notes on his lectern.

"Let's see. Dolores Olson and Sandy Silence. Is that right?" They agreed. Then, taking a good look at them, he asked, "Why are you here together? Are you sisters?"

They laughed and said, "No."

"Brothers?" Groucho pursued. They giggled. "Why are you here together?"

Neither one of them having any answer, Dolores took a wild stab. "Well, Mr. Fidderman thought...."

Groucho, startled, said, "What was that?"

"Mr. Fidderman...." She tried to continue, but Groucho's instincts were aroused.

"Mr. Fidderman? What show is he connected with?" Dolores was obviously baffled. "You mean Fenneman?" He was on to something. "Did he tell you his name was Fidderman?" He called offstage. "Hey, Fidderman, come out here!"

Fenneman entered with an expression that was a mixture of amusement, embarrassment, and apprehension. He was openly delighted with the challenge of working with Groucho and terrified of the pitfalls. His typical remark, which I heard him say as he passed me on his way onstage, was, simply, a fervent, "Oh, boy!" He took his customary place between Groucho and the young women.

Groucho greeted him with, "You've changed your name, I see. Have you been doing this for a long time?"

"Doing what?" George said, cautiously.

"Using two names," Groucho insisted. "Why did you call yourself Fidderman when you met these two girls? You knew they'd find out your name is Fenneman. Why did you do this, George?"

Since he actually never had done it, George, not surprisingly, had no answer. His only tactic was to use the public personality he had created for his role on the show, which was, in reality, pretty close to his own.

"I didn't do anything, honest!"

Groucho now adopted an air of sweet reason. "They told me you said your name is Fidderman. Now, you must have been doing it for some reason. When I use a different name there's a reason for it. Aren't you a married man?"

"Up until now I was, yes!"

It was a rare departure from his self-imposed rule never to make a deliberate joke, and, above all, never to try to top Groucho.

"I very seldom tried to outsmart him," George said to me years later. "Once in a while I thought, 'I'm going to do it, to hell with 'em.' And I would get a laugh I shouldn't have. I didn't get many of those. I could best him by being myself—the underdog. You become the favorite. It made my life and my career."

On this occasion, however, Groucho was not to be distracted. He relentlessly pursued the subject of the two women. "How did you find out they were roommates?" Fenneman's dilemma deepened. In fact, he really didn't know anything about the two young women. All his information about them came from the script, which gave only their names.

They had been discovered by one of our staff of people finders who had learned from talking to both of them that they were roommates who had both experienced endless difficulties in holding steady jobs. Since they were attractive and talkative, Bernie Smith had decided that Groucho could have some fun with them if they appeared together. Just before the show, someone on our staff had casually suggested to them that if Groucho were to ask how they happened to be here together, they might say that George had invited them. No one bothered to tell George.

Now the audience and Groucho were having a lovely time, in spite of, or perhaps because of, George's obvious discomfort, and especially in the light of his well-established All American Boy image. Groucho continued with an air of benign patience.

"George, I'm not criticizing you. I just want to know what technique you use, that's all."

Fenneman had no idea what the Fidderman ploy was about. He suspected a more complicated plot and didn't want to spoil it. He took a chance and fabricated what seemed to be a simple explanation.

"Actually, a friend of mine told me about the girls, and...."

It merely gave Groucho another line of attack. "A friend of yours knew these girls, and he introduced you to them?"

"Well, actually he told me about them...." George gave up. "I wasn't even there!"

Groucho recognized the end of a routine when he heard it. "Oh, the old line, 'The light that lies in a man's eyes and lies and lies and lies!' Well, there it is, folks, the private life of George Fidderman!"

Fenneman knew an exit cue, too, and took it.

For the record, I submit that in 1950 it was politically correct to refer to young women as girls.

On a later program, in 1954, the first pair of contestants had played the game and made their exit. Fenneman moved to his microphone to introduce the next couple. The cameras continued to roll, and the sound was being recorded. Groucho had a small antic inspiration.

"All right Gheorgh," he said, using what he imagined was the French pronunciation of George, "who's next?"

"Groucho..." George began.

"Gheorgh," Groucho said. "That's French."

"Yes," George said, with a slight hesitation, "I can tell." With a look at Groucho, he waited a moment, decided it was safe to continue. "We have a man from the Los Angeles Chamber...."

"I always call you George," Groucho said, "but I thought I'd call you Gheorgh tonight. You like that?"

"That's nice of you," George said politely, and paused again, in case Groucho had more. "We have a ...."

"It doesn't cost me anything." Groucho was searching, not willing to let go just yet. "I get it wholesale."

Since there was almost no audience response, George felt safe in continuing, but he changed the wording slightly, hoping to remind Groucho that there was some business to tend to. "There's a man waiting out here...."

"With a black mustache?" Groucho pounced like a hawk. At last he had a hook. "We had a joke like that in one of our shows. My brother comes in and says, 'There's a man outside, wants to see you with a black mustache.' And I say, 'Well, tell him I've got one.'" The audience was amused, but moderately. "Well, this was 1929. Things were different in those days."

"There's a man outside...." George persisted, then realized that if he didn't change the construction, the routine might go on indefinitely. "Let me start from the other end. This man's partner is Miss Rene Gretch, and the man waiting is from the Los Angeles Chamber of Commerce, Mr. Richard Pollis. Will you come in and meet Groucho Marx?"

In December 1955, Groucho had another gambit.

GROUCHO:	Well, here I am again with a thousand dollars for one of our couplays. Is that right, couplay?
FENNEMAN:	That may be the French pronunciation—or not.
GROUCHO:	What's correct?
FENNEMAN:	Couples is probably it.
GROUCHO:	Oh. George, who's first on the agenda? Is that right, agenda?
FENNEMAN:	Agenda, yes.
GROUCHO:	What does that mean?
FENNEMAN:	List.
GROUCHO:	I've got a little agenda, from Gilbert & Sullivan—would you say that? *(Sings.)* As someday it may happen that a victim must be found, I've got a little agenda.[1] That doesn't make sense!

Betsy Drake (ex-Mrs. Cary Grant) and George Fenneman in 1958 when George was M.C. of his own show *The Perfect Husband.* **(Courtesy Paul Wesolowski)**

FENNEMAN: Roster.

GROUCHO: Roster? That's a male chicken, a roster. You know when Franz Liszt was born, that's what his mother sang—"I've got a little Liszt." Who's first, George?

Never heard on the air were the problems George had in getting the show started at all. When we were ready to go, Groucho would have just finished about 10 minutes of fooling around with the audience, getting them in the mood for laughter, telling stories, perhaps singing a song and, finally, interrupting me while I tried to explain to the audience why they should not attempt to help in the quiz by supplying answers. At last, I concentrated on watching Groucho, trying to guess when he felt like starting. George was ready, waiting for my cue to say, "Ladies and gentlemen, the secret word tonight is ....."

FENNEMAN: *(To me.)* All right?
DWAN: Okay.
GROUCHO: I'm on another show Monday night, if you're near a radio. It's called *The Railroad Hour*.

(Pause. I cue George.)

FENNEMAN: Ladies and gentlemen.....
GROUCHO: *(To me.)* Anything else you want to tell them?
DWAN: No.

(Pause. I cue George.)

FENNEMAN: Ladies....
GROUCHO: *(Sings.)* Brush your teeth with Colgate, Colgate dental cream.
               (Shouts.) What a toothpaste!
               Love that commercial. That's on the show George does in the afternoon. Show them your teeth, George. *(George smiles.)* No, take them out and pass them around!
               Okay, let's go ahead with this folderol.
DWAN: Are you ready?
GROUCHO: I'm ready. I've been ready for hours. Are you going to spell it tonight, George?
FENNEMAN: *(Rapidly.)* Ladies and gentlemen, the secret word tonight is table, T-A-B-L-E.
GROUCHO: Really?
FENNEMAN: You Bet Your Life!

Fenneman's afternoon show that Groucho mentioned, the one with the Colgate commercial, was the basis for a possible rift, but it never became a serious problem. It was a program called *The Perfect Husband*, with George as master of ceremonies. In that it was a quiz show with

Fenneman and Groucho (Courtesy Paul Wesolowski)

George engaging in some chatter with the guests, it bore a considerable resemblance to *You Bet Your Life*. But the major difficulty arose when

This original still reads: Groucho (with cigar) and George Fenneman return with the former's high-rated comedy quiz program for another year on the NBC-TV network, Thursday nights, and on the NBC Radio Network Monday nights. Groucho's quips and quizzes and George's scorekeeping have highlighted the series on TV for nine years and on radio for 13 (fall, 1959). (Photofest) Once again this proves you can't trust studio publicity; the show was on the radio only 6 years.

George made what he later considered a terrible mistake. He hired the Russell Birdwell office as publicists. They put out a series of stories in which they referred to George as "the host" of *You Bet Your Life*. Groucho mentioned this casually, but with some displeasure, at one of our meetings, and Bernie told George. Groucho never said anything directly to George, but the Russell Birdwell office was dropped from Fenneman's employ.

George continued to do *The Perfect Husband* for more than a year and, in fact, did several others during the years—a panel show called *Claim to Fame*, with Vincent Price, a program featuring home movies, entitled *Funny, Funny Films* (an amusing program created by *You Bet Your Life* writer Hy Freedman, but ahead of its time), and a show called *Surprise Package*, on which Harpo made a guest appearance. John Guedel was also constantly promoting George for a show of his own and did manage to sell him in *Anybody Can Play*, which tried to reach out to the home audience but was also ahead of its time as an interactive vehicle. It lasted 26 weeks.

George was also on the air very frequently but anonymously. He was the voice at the beginning of another leading program that said, "*Gunsmoke*, brought to you by Chesterfield. They satisfy." And, perhaps most memorably, his were the resonant tones that opened every episode of *Dragnet*. "The story you are about to hear is true. Only the names have been changed to protect the innocent."

Fenneman also made a few movies—supporting roles in *How to Succeed in Business Without Really Trying* and in what is now a cult picture, a science fiction horror film, *The Thing*, and he had the lead in an obscure entry, *Mystery Lake*. He freely acknowledges that his best role was as Groucho's right-hand man on *You Bet Your Life*.

George had been aware of Groucho and, in some ways, had been preparing for the working relationship for many years before *You Bet Your Life*. He talked to me over lunch near his home in the San Fernando Valley in the spring of 1991. He did a better than average Groucho imitation with an imaginary cigar and hyperactive eyebrows. He remembered:

> Groucho was my hero when I was in high school. I did all the shtick. "Send up three dozen roses to Mrs. Rittenhouse and write 'I love you' on the back of the bill." I'd seen him with the brothers live on stage in San Francisco when they were touring *A Day at the Races* before making the movie. We'd go early to the Golden Gate Theatre and sit through three shows a day. I saw poor Margaret Dumont get papered into the wall over and over again.

(Groucho once told George that he filled the same role in the television show that Margaret Dumont did in the movies.)

I first met George around 1940 when he was a student at San Francisco State College, and I was a youthful Program Director for the radio station KGO and the ABC network in San Francisco. He and his friend, Bob Sweeney, brought me a comedy panel show called *Profs Are Human* in which Fenneman and Sweeney used farcical dramatizations of quiz questions not only to baffle a panel of their professors but also as on-the-air auditions for George and Bob as sketch performers. I remember that the show was pretty funny but somewhat offbeat for the conventional San Francisco radio of the 1940s.

After graduation from college, Fenneman came to work for me in San Francisco as a staff announcer for ABC and KGO. He later transferred to the ABC staff in Hollywood. By that time, I had moved to Hollywood, too, and we met one day late in 1946 at the corner of Selma and Vine Streets—historic, also, as the site of the first Hollywood motion picture studio. I told George about the auditions we were holding that afternoon for the announcer on the new Groucho Marx radio program. He could squeeze 15 minutes out of his schedule as announcer on KABC radio, and I agreed to schedule him first so he could run up the street to the audition studio at Hollywood and Vine.

Hiring the announcer was the producer's prerogative, not the director's, but I knew then that Fenneman was the man I wanted for the show. There was no idea, then, of casting a foil for Groucho. The announcer's primary duties would be to deliver the commercials for Elgin American Compacts, but we also needed someone to keep track of the score in the quiz. Many a mellifluous, resonant voice came from a voice box that continued to the back of the skull with scarcely any interference from brain tissue. George, I knew, had a voice *and* brains. He won the audition as commercial announcer, but producer John Guedel cast Jack Slattery as program announcer and to work with Groucho in the quiz. John knew he could rely on Jack since he was Art Linkletter's announcer on the Guedel production, *House Party*, five days a week on CBS, where he had convincingly proved not only that he was an attractive radio personality, but also that he could think on his feet.

On the first program, Fenneman read the commercials for Elgin American Compacts into a separate microphone at the side of the stage. To close the first pitch, the copy called for him to say, "Ladies, have you looked at your compact lately?" George gave it the full treatment.

He leaned into the microphone, adopted an unctuous bedroom tone, and delivered the line as a sort of veiled invitation.

Groucho said, "Who was that?," left his stool and lectern and joined Fenneman at his microphone.

"I was terrified," George said later. "We were being recorded, but every other radio program at that time was broadcast live, every word scripted and approved. Everything that was said went immediately on the air and into homes all across the country. That was my whole training. Now, here I was confronted by my hero, and he wanted to talk—without a script!"

Groucho said, "Do you always talk like that?"

George told me later in carefully chosen words, "I got the impression that he was challenging my manhood. I didn't know exactly how to respond, but I had the good luck to do one thing right. Whatever it was I said, it gave him a chance to respond. He must have liked my attitude, because we talked for quite a while."

Groucho recognized the potential. By the third session, Fenneman was the program announcer and stayed in that role for 14 years.

His regular duties on radio were, first, to identify the secret word and the name of the program for the radio audience.

FENNEMAN: *(Confidentially.)* Ladies and gentlemen, the secret word tonight is chair, C H A I R.
GROUCHO: Really?
FENNEMAN: You Bet Your Life!
ORCHESTRA: "HOORAY FOR CAPTAIN SPAULDING" (From *Animal Crackers.*)

After identifying the sponsor (simpler in those times because we had only one at a time), Fenneman's next important task was to introduce Groucho with the familiar, "And here he is, the one, the only...." The studio audience would dutifully, but apparently happily, respond by shouting in unison, "Groucho!" Groucho would counter in mock surprise with "Oh, that's me!" and the show was under way.

Introducing the contestants was Fenneman's next duty, moments always pregnant with the possibility of interruption. It was Groucho's first chance to practice some freewheeling improvisation, to engage, occasionally, in a bit of George-baiting. Once the guests were introduced, however, and were safely on stage, George made his exit and stayed off

(Courtesy Paul Wesolowski)

until it was time to play *You Bet Your Life*. It was an accidental result of the format that George appeared only at the beginning and end of each segment. But it worked to his advantage. When Groucho summoned him onstage at other times, it was a special occasion, usually containing some sort of challenge. Bernie Smith also used George occasionally for something that called for advance preparation or where a contestant might not be expected to agree to participate. There was the unplanned

As Long As They're Laughing

occasion when a buxom lady wrestler, at Groucho's urging, used one of her wrestling holds—in non-technical terms, a bear hug—to lift George clear off the stage.

"I had my knees in her bosom," George remembers. "It was embarrassing."

Fenneman did not enjoy physical contact. When George was the announcer on the *Martin and Lewis Show* on radio, Jerry Lewis was a notorious low comedy manhandler. George said:

> Jerry was very physical. Dick Stabile was the orchestra leader, and Jerry would cut off his tie with a scissors, pull his coat down and rip off the lapels. Of course, then he gave him a new jacket and tie.
>
> On the first show I was on, he grabbed me by the tie and pulled me up like he was hanging me. I laughed, because we were in front of an audience. When the show was over, I said, "Jerry, don't ever touch me again. You can talk to me, but don't ever touch me, or so help me, I'll punch you right in the mouth in front of the audience and everyone. You can punch me back, but I'll punch you first." He never did touch me again. I think I gained some respect.

He did allow some liberties on our show, trusting Bernie Smith's judgment to protect his dignity and physical well-being. Bernie pushed him to the limit in the segment with Peter Foy, the man behind Mary Martin's magical flying in the theatrical staging of *Peter Pan*. Peter developed the harness and special rigging, and he and his crew controlled the operation that made the spectacular levitation so effective.

To follow Groucho's interview with Peter, a demonstration was inevitable. Preparation ahead of time was necessary, and George reluctantly agreed to do it, relying on the experience and professionalism of Peter and his staff. We had to buy an extra-large pair of trousers to fit over the harness and to match Fenneman's otherwise impeccable attire. The pants were thereafter worthless since several sizable holes had to be cut for the wires.

All went well with the demonstration. George swooped triumphantly across the rear stage opening, six feet off the ground, wearing an expression of astonished delight. Suddenly, something went wrong with his balance, and he made the next four or five trips across the stage in an upside-down vertical position, legs thrashing above, his head pointing to the floor.

There were other unplanned hazards, one involving the duck. On one occasion, the secret word was said during the quiz. George was standing on his regular spot between Groucho and the guests. The stage hand turned the bird loose, letting it drop to the full length of its rigging, just enough to hit George squarely on top of his head. The word, by coincidence, was "HAT."

George faced the challenge of the quiz three times in each program. It seemed a simple task, and it was, barring extraneous complications, some of which were of Mr. Marx's invention. It was George's task to explain the quiz rules to the contestants, and each time he did it, whether the 54th or the 254th, it was informal and informative, not a mechanical rote. On a February night in 1952, Groucho started the proceedings as follows:

GROUCHO: All right, here we go. Let's see how high you can build your $20. How much do you want to bet?

FENNEMAN: Do you want me to explain the rules to them first?

GROUCHO: Well, yes, if you care to.

FENNEMAN: All right.

GROUCHO: And talk slowly until I get this stogie going.

FENNEMAN: All right. You bet as much of your $20....

GROUCHO: Slower.

FENNEMAN: (Slowly.) You bet as much of your $20....

GROUCHO: Slower.

FENNEMAN: You take your $20....

GROUCHO: Faster.

FENNEMAN: (Faster.) You bet as much of your $20 as you want.

GROUCHO: Faster, Fenneman. I'm all lit, here.

FENNEMAN: ...on each of four questions, you see, and then (laughs) I forget the rules!

George's primary concern was to keep the score. In its basic form, the game of *You Bet Your Life,* as invented by John Guedel, gave each couple $20. They could bet as much of their bankroll as they chose on each of four questions. George had to have two numbers ready—one from addition in case of a right answer, the other from subtraction in case they were wrong—calculated while the couple was agreeing on a single answer. That was the theory. But Groucho was not a harsh quizmaster. As soon as either contestant gave the right answer, he gave the verdict. George had to be fast and accurate. That was not too difficult if the bets were in round numbers.

George, however, remembered:

> Groucho was supposed to say to them, "Bet as much of your hundred dollars as you want." He would encourage them to bet $37.27. And the damn fools would do it! If they got it right, it was simple. "Now they have $137.27! Now bet as much of that as you want." They would bet $42.10. I haven't even started to add or subtract, and they have the right answer!
>
> But it worked to my advantage, because he kept calling me stupid, and there I was, the underdog again. He had me going to Stanford, because, he said, "At Stanford they have special math courses where they teach them to be stupid!" Of course, I didn't go to Stanford, I graduated from San Francisco State, and when I tried to correct him, he wouldn't hear any excuses.
>
> After a while, my friends from San Francisco State began to needle me, "How come you're claiming you went to Stanford?" So one night I explained to Groucho and asked him if he would please straighten it out on the air—that it wasn't me, but Bob Dwan who went to Stanford. He was very nice about it, and on the next

program he said, "George, I understand you've been lying about where you went to school." That helped me a lot with my friends, but it made another nice sequence for the show.

The offbeat betting reached its peak in March 1952, when one of our guests was Robert Crawford, a high-school mathematics teacher, who said his students called him Uncle Fred. He did all the betting, and his partner, Virginia Ryan, a telephone operator, knew all the answers. (The previous couple, which included Los Angeles City Councilman Kenneth Hahn, had bet high and had accumulated $298, which put them in the lead for a chance at the final big question, worth $2,000 that night.)

GROUCHO: All right, let's see how high you can build your $20. You selected husband and wife teams on radio and television. How much of your $20 will you bet?

TEACHER: Nineteen dollars and fifty-two cents.

GROUCHO: One of the most popular husband and wife teams on radio actually used their own kids, Ricky and David, on their show. What is the name of this popular team?

WOMAN: Ozzie and Harriet.

GROUCHO: Ozzie and Harriet is right.

FENNEMAN: You're off to a good start. You have $39.52!

GROUCHO: How much of the $39.52 are you going to bet?

TEACHER: Thirty-nine dollars?

GROUCHO: Oh, make it tough on yourself. You're a math teacher. Make it $39 and eight-and-a-half cents.

TEACHER: Thirty-nine dollars, 40 cents, and two mills.

GROUCHO: And don't forget, the mills of the gods grind slowly!

FENNEMAN: Now what's he going to bet?

GROUCHO: Don't let him talk you out of it.

TEACHER: Thirty-nine dollars, 40 cents, and two mills.

GROUCHO: That's right. George is allegedly a graduate of the University of San Francisco, he ought to know that. Who played the leading roles in *The Halls of Ivy*?

WOMAN: Ronald Coleman and his wife Benita.

FENNEMAN: You have....

GROUCHO:	*(To teacher.)* Just a moment. How much have you got?
TEACHER:	Seventy-eight ninety-two, two.
FENNEMAN:	Exactly what I have.
GROUCHO:	And I had it right on the tip of my tongue. How much will you bet?
TEACHER:	Seventy-eight dollars and ninety cents.
GROUCHO:	And no centimes?
TEACHER:	That's good enough.
GROUCHO:	What is the name of the couple who lives in Wistful Vista?
WOMAN:	Fibber McGee and Molly.
GROUCHO:	Right. How much have you got, Fred?
TEACHER:	Let's see, I lost track.
FENNEMAN:	*(Triumphantly.)* *I've* got it! You have $157.82 and two of those mills.
GROUCHO:	Now they have four mills. They have the Mills Brothers. Here's your last chance to beat the other couples. How much will you bet?
TEACHER:	We'll bet $157.81.
GROUCHO:	*I Love Lucy* stars a husband and wife team. What are their names?
WOMAN:	Lucille Ball and Desi Arnaz.
FENNEMAN:	You wind up with $315.63 and four mills and a chance at the $2,000 question!

Unfortunately, they didn't know that the *Graf Spee* was the ship scuttled off the coast of Uruguay in World War II, so they didn't win the $2,000.

The relationship between George and Groucho emerged gradually. It was not part of an overall plan to develop Fenneman as the standard sidekick so common on other shows. It is a good example of one of the great advantages we had over almost every other comedy show, then, or later. No one on our staff had to be assigned each week to write the "Groucho-George sketch." We were able to rely on Groucho and George to make the most of the material at hand.

George Fenneman in 1991

George did very well after *You Bet Your Life*. He hosted several educational programs on PBS, was a much sought-after commercial announcer, and finally was placed under contract by Home Savings & Loan to be their on-air spokesman and general ambassador of good will. He traveled through the west to open new bank branches and going on cruises with their bonus prize winners. He remained what he always was—a very bright and witty man with a wonderful voice and impeccable diction, a good friend and a gentleman. I regret to report that he died on May 29, 1997, at the age of 77.

(Courtesy Paul Wesolowski)

As Long As They're Laughing

CHAPTER 11
On the Road

Time For Elizabeth is a play written by Groucho and his close friend, Norman Krasna. We toured it on the summer theatre circuit for four summers between 1957 and 1963. The play was originally written around 1936, under the title, *The Middle Ages.* It was inspired by a magazine advertisement Groucho saw promoting the glories of Florida retirement, with "care-free days spent golfing and catching swordfish." It is a gentle satire on the dreams of upper-middle-class retirement subjected to the realities of a lower-middle-class environment. It tells the story of Ed Davis, general manager of a washing machine factory, who is weary of the all-consuming demands of his job and especially of the tyranny of his mean-spirited boss, the factory owner. He throws it all up and flees to Florida with his loyal, patient, and devoted wife, only to discover that retirement is not all it's cracked up to be. The new and somewhat mysterious title, *Time For Elizabeth,* incidentally, refers to the town of Elizabeth, New Jersey, where a retiring employee plans to spend his golden years. His decision triggers Ed Davis' resolve. It is about as predictable as it sounds, but it is a well-constructed, conventional play—Norman Krasna was a highly professional playwright and a prolific screenwriter. He was a four-time Academy Award nominee and won the Oscar for his original screenplay for *Princess O'Rourke,* starring Olivia DeHavilland. He had 10 plays on Broadway, including *Dear Ruth*, roughly based on life in the Groucho Marx household.

The authors of *Time For Elizabeth* did, I think, misjudge the social climate of the times. Early retirement was not a burning issue in mid-Depression 1936, and hardly more so 20 years later.

When Groucho reread *The Middle Ages* in 1946, he persuaded Norman Krasna to undertake a rewrite with him:

I may appear in it, if it works out. I told
Norman I wouldn't consider two years in
it, but, if it were good, I'd play a year in
New York, if necessary. [1]

Then began the long process of rewriting. It was no token collaboration just to get Groucho's name above the title. In April 1947 he wrote to Miriam:

...I am working hard with Krasna, and
we have thrown out practically the whole
second act and have started from scratch
again. This is the fourth time we have done
this play, and it's now been ten years since
we started it. [2]

Even as late as June 1948, just a week before the cast was scheduled to begin rehearsing in San Francisco, they were still unhappy with the second act and started another rewrite.

One thing had been firmly settled. Groucho had abandoned his notion of playing the lead role:

Appearing on stage every night for a year
doesn't strike me as much of an existence. [3]

For a time, they thought they had Fredric March and his wife Florence Eldredge interested, but finally cast a fine actor, Otto Kruger, in the role:

It's astonishing how many people dislike
this play, but Krasna and I are putting
our own money in it as a gesture of nose-
thumbing defiance. [4]

Time For Elizabeth played two weeks in San Francisco, two weeks at the Biltmore Theatre in Los Angeles, and then moved to the Fulton Theatre in New York, where it opened and quickly closed.

October 9, 1948:

As Long As They're Laughing

...it was certainly nice to get out of New York and those reviews. I am just beginning to recover from the effects of the pannings. I had no idea how deeply it had left its scars. Fortunately, I am so busy, I have very little time to brood about them or the play. I think the critics are unfair, bigoted bastards....[5]

Miriam Marx Allen appends a footnote.

My father always wanted to be a writer—far more than he wanted to be a comedian—so it was a great disappointment to him when his play flopped on Broadway.[6]

He wrote a letter not for publication to Abel Green, editor of *Variety*, in November:

I am slowly recovering from the lacing we received from the New York critics.... Lardner, in the *Star*, lampooned me because I had co-authored a play that wasn't sardonic, sarcastic, or brittle. Krutch, in the *Nation*, chided me for departing from the character I always portrayed on the screen and stage.... Judging from the fury with which most of the critics attack the author, one would think that presenting a play in New York was a criminal offense.[7]

One more thing remained to be proved, however—that the play might have been a success with Groucho in the lead. There's an interesting counter-irony in the fact that if Groucho had signed on to play New York for a year in 1947, he would not have been able to do *You Bet Your Life,* and 1948 might have been a year of defeat rather than triumph.

By 1952, with *You Bet Your Life* in its fifth year, and a success, he had enough confidence to give appearing in *Time For Elizabeth* a small try. With the encouragement of Norman Krasna, he agreed to appear in the play for one week at the La Jolla Playhouse near San Diego. His son Arthur wrote in 1954:

> Whether *Time for Elizabeth* was a better play with Father in it, or whether audiences just wanted to see him on stage again, is debatable. However, his one-week engagement there was the outstanding success of La Jolla's summer stock season. The management had to schedule two extra matinees to take care of all the customers who had been turned away from the regular showings. *Time for Elizabeth* probably could have played to capacity all summer... if Father had been willing, which he wasn't.... I realized why after watching him do the show every night.... At one spot in the third act, the action called for Father to stretch out on a couch, say a few lines, then stand up again.... When the cue came for him to get up again, he didn't budge. In fact, he remained on the couch for about five extra pages of dialogue....[8]

La Jolla demonstrated that the play would work with Groucho in it, but he still had the bug to prove it further. He had played summer stock in 1934, appearing in a "straw hat" theatre in Maine in *Twentieth Century,* and he remembered it as a pleasant experience. In 1957, with *You Bet Your Life* in its 10th year, he decided to try it again. Gummo, through theatrical agent Frances Hidden in New York, negotiated contracts with two summer theatres. Groucho, with Krasna's approval, asked me to direct. We would open in the remote and charming Paper Mill Playhouse run by Harold J. Kennedy in Millburn, New Jersey, upstate, near the Delaware Gap, and play a second week on the coast at the Theatre by the Sea in Matunuck, Rhode Island. We went to New York to cast the play with the help of Frances Hidden, and managed to line up a first-rate cast. I suppose it sounded like an adventure, touring with Groucho Marx, and we had no trouble lining up candidates. Groucho was very sensitive

The stage version of *Time For Elizabeth*, summer 1958, at the Westport Country Playhouse, Westport, Connecticut. Groucho as Ed Davis, Wyatt Cooper as his son-in-law, Elizabeth Tilton as his daughter, and Kathy Eames as his wife. (Courtesy Paul Wesolowski)

about actors' feelings and hated rejecting anyone. Several of them were surprised to receive phone calls apologizing for not casting them. We did get a wonderful actress, Nancy Sheridan, to play the wife. Unfortunately, she wasn't free to play the subsequent seasons, but her successor, Kathy Eames, who played Kay Davis the other three years and in the television version we later made, was equally charming and compatible.

Groucho also had a chance to visit his old haunts in New York, especially Dinty Moore's Restaurant for lunch, where the highlight of the week was having a table adjacent to the playwrights, Lindsay and Crouse. He found that times had changed, however, when he tried his daily walk around the block from the Astor Hotel. Previously, when working in New York, he could sally forth without his theatrical makeup and stroll undisturbed. Now, after six years on national television in his natural guise, when he ventured out he ran a gauntlet of autograph seekers and well wishers, and he had to give it up, confining himself to his room and the *New York Times*.

The tour was not one long round of fun and games and mad escapades as the popular fantasy might be of a trip with one of the Marx Brothers. Groucho was serious about the task at hand, determined to prove his competency as an actor, and the cast was a bunch of professionals. Groucho was unquestionably the star, and was treated as such—some of the perks being carefully written into the contract that Gummo had negotiated. It was a family affair. Groucho's wife Eden and daughter Melinda were on the tour. Eden, a reasonably competent actress, played the role of the secretary the first season and then was promoted to the still small, but crucial, role of the femme fatale. She looked the part. I took one of my teenagers on each tour, partly as company for Melinda. It was as much a new experience for me as it was for them, and I loved every minute of it. Directing for the stage was a totally different challenge from directing *You Bet Your Life,* and it was truly stimulating. I also acted as company manager, keeper of accounts, and press relations officer. The latter job I handled with uneven success. On one of our trips to England, I managed to alienate the entire British press corps, who were, at least in the 1950s, a ruthless bunch, by saying in exasperation that since interviewing was Groucho's business he didn't grant free interviews at the drop of a hat. That was a mistake.

Groucho enjoyed being part of a theatrical troupe again. Here is a brief monologue I overheard when he was speaking to a group of players backstage at the Sombrero Theatre in Phoenix, Arizona.

Hans Conried had just finished a skillful and charming performance that ended his season of touring in *Critic's Choice.* We were to follow him in our production of *Time For Elizabeth.* Groucho said:

> I hate to see a theatrical company break up.
> It's like being on shipboard. A camaraderie
> develops, relationships are established.
> Last summer on the way to Hawaii, I had
> two priests almost persuaded to give the
> whole thing up and try some other line of
> work, when we sighted land. I am very
> persuasive on shipboard because there
> is nothing else to do. Oh, I tried jump-
> ing overboard a couple of times, but they
> talked me out of that.

The speech is also a lovely example of the way his mind worked in dealing with sentiment and then quickly taking the first exit at the merest hint of sentimentality.

He was warmly, affectionately, received by audiences on the summer circuit. Financially, it was a big success, breaking box-office records by selling out wherever we played. Who could resist the chance to see Groucho in person at a summer resort? How well the theatres did, I am not sure, since Groucho, or Gummo, drove a hard bargain in negotiating for his fee.

The main problem with the play was that it was not what an audience who came to see Groucho expected to see. At the most, they expected something like the clown of *Animal Crackers* or, at the least, the iconoclastic jokester of *You Bet Your Life*. But Groucho's main reason for appearing in the play was to prove that he could play a straight, legitimate role. He always insisted that it is much more difficult to play comedy than drama because the audience verdict was immediate in comedy. Any good comedian, he contended, should have no difficulty playing a serious role. So Groucho played Ed Davis straight most of the time, and played him well. The audience reaction was friendly, but slightly baffled. The most successful part of the performances was always his 20-minute afterpiece in which he became Groucho, the raconteur.

The local newspaper reviews were respectful, if not wildly enthusiastic:

> Anyone within hearing distance of the Lakes Region Playhouse last night knew that the audience was having a rare evening, for the laughter was so spontaneous and so frequent.—Laconia, New Hampshire, *Evening Citizen,* July 8, 1958

> ...people are telling their friends what an enjoyable evening they had....—*The Saratogian,* Saratoga Springs, N.Y., July 14, 1959

> Groucho Marx is a good-humor man, *cum laude*. It's a cunning summer vehicle for

> Groucho, an unpretentious combination of
> malarkey and good sense. —*Chicago Sun
> Times,* July 21, 1959

It did not bring joy to the troupe or its star, however, when one of the deans of the reviewing profession, Elliot Norton, ventured up to New Hampshire to report for a Boston paper:

> ...in a poor play called *Time For Eliza-beth,* Groucho Marx is often extremely funny. —*Boston Sunday Advertiser,* July 13, 1958

In 1958, we ventured north to The Lakes Region Playhouse at Lake Winnipesaukee in Laconia, New Hampshire, then to the Ivoryton Playhouse in Ivoryton, Connecticut, and finally to the class of the circuit, the Westport Country Playhouse in Westport, Connecticut. Groucho especially enjoyed that booking because some of his old cronies came up from New York to see the performance. He stayed in the home of the legendary theatrical agent, Audrey Wood, and his visitors included Alastair Cooke, Goddard Lieberson, Betty Comden, and Adolph Green.

In 1959, we played Saratoga Springs, New York, and the Edgewater Beach Hotel in Chicago, where they had set up a large tent on the lawn in the rear of the hotel. I remember that the hotel manager met us personally at the airport and announced with considerable pride that he had arranged for Groucho to be delivered directly to the hotel in a helicopter. He was greatly taken aback to find that Groucho was furious. In the first place, he didn't like the idea of leaving the rest of the troupe to be transported in a bus like second-class citizens. But mostly, he was appalled at the idea of the helicopter. He was finally persuaded to take the ride, but he was terrified the whole way. He couldn't sleep that night (not uncommon with him before an opening) and had to call the house doctor at two a.m. for some kind of a potion. He was fine, as usual, for the performance, but that day it rained all day in Chicago, and by the evening the tent was leaking badly, especially over the first 10 rows. In the middle of the first act, Groucho rushed down into the house with an armful of towels. "First you get soaked at the box-office," he said, "and then you get soaked in here."

When we played Phoenix and Tucson, Arizona, in 1963, several things were different. *You Bet Your Life* was still in reruns, but we had not done any new shows for two years. Both cities were retirement locations and might have been expected to have some sympathy toward the theme of the play, but neither city was a summer resort in the sense that most of the eastern locations had been. The Sombrero Theatre in Phoenix was a quite high-minded community theatre, and its patrons had somewhat different expectations of the theatre than the "straw hat" patrons.

Groucho began to fool around a little. Not within the body of the play, but around the edges. Early in the second act, Ed Davis and his wife were eating one of the first meals she had prepared since their arrival in Florida. Ed calmly but firmly announced that he didn't like carrots.

"They're good for you," his wife said. "Helps you see in the dark."

"If I want to see in the dark," Groucho said following the script, "I'll eat what a cat does. Mice!"

However, after his wife had gone back to the kitchen, Ed took the bowl of carrots and dumped the contents in a dresser drawer. The audience was slightly baffled, but delighted. After the performance, Groucho said to me, "Get me a rabbit for tomorrow night."

"A live rabbit?"

"Yes."

"But, Groucho," I said, "that doesn't make sense!"

"As long as they're laughing," he said.

I got the rabbit, and the next night, we kept it backstage. Groucho said nothing about it until after the curtain fell on the third act. Then he got the rabbit, and returning for his curtain call, carried it across the stage and put it in the drawer with the carrots.

Anything for a laugh? Not quite. It was, of course, essentially the way he had worked with his brothers from the beginning—try something, if it gets a laugh, keep it in, if it doesn't, cut it out and try something else.

Things went steadily downhill in Tucson, although there was one highlight when Thornton Wilder came to see the play. He was affable, pleasantly cautious in his comments on the play. At dinner afterward, Groucho had me seated next to Mr. Wilder. I asked some leading questions and learned that he was working on the adaptation of one of his plays into a musical to be called *Hello, Dolly!*

"And what have you been doing, young man?" I couldn't think of a single thing.

We played The Temple of Music and Art, next door to a mortuary, and one afternoon we realized that there were more people in the funeral parlor than were in our matinee audience. After the show, Groucho suddenly decided he needed a roll of paper towels for his dressing room. Ignoring the supermarket, he tried a laundry, a hardware store, the Post Office, and a shoe repair shop, asking in each place for paper towels. Failing in that quest, he decided that an acceptable substitute would be hot-cross buns. Unfortunately, most of the people he stopped on the street were Spanish-speaking. His objective was, therefore, switched to finding a Spanish dictionary. In a perverse reversal of his normal logic, he tried a book store, and, after asking for hot-cross buns, finally found a pocket English-Spanish dictionary. Opening the small volume, he selected the first word that looked familiar, "elephante." He walked the two blocks back to the hotel, stopping passersby and asking, "Elephante?" and finally retired to his room, without paper towels, hot-cross buns, or elephants, to read the *New York Times*.

The next morning, we took a long walk through the quiet streets of Tucson. "Why are you doing this to yourself?" I asked. "You've proved what you set out to prove."

I never did receive a satisfactory answer to that question. Here was a man who had achieved the pinnacle in the theatre, movies, radio and television, touring in a play that wasn't very good, getting poor notices and slim houses, and apparently enjoying it. There in Tuscon he did agree that the tour would end, and we never took the show on the road again. But *Time For Elizabeth* was not dead yet; it had one more incarnation yet to come. Groucho couldn't resist the chance to play it on television, and in 1964 it was presented in a one-hour version on the *Chrysler Theatre*. I made the adaptation to Groucho's satisfaction, and the program was directed by Ezra Stone. We brought Kathy Eames out from New York to play the wife, as she had in summer stock, but there was one other bit of casting that seems odd in retrospect. A young and handsome Dennis Hopper played the very straight role of the son-in-law.

The only thing that kept the show from really working was Groucho's insistence on relying on cue cards. In spite of the fact that he had written the lines himself in the first place and had played them dozens of times onstage, he was still nervous about getting the abbreviated version right. Reading from the cards, unfortunately, imposed a considerable stiffness on his performance, only making the contrast to his old movie roles more noticeable.

Eden Marx, Groucho and Kathryn Eames from the telecast of *Time For Elizabeth*
April 24, 1964. (Courtesy Paul Wesolowski)

But even after the television show, he kept dreaming. He wrote to
Norman Krasna on the day he finished shooting the TV film:

> As you know, I have tried for years to
> interest a studio in converting this into a
> movie.... If the TV episode is very good,
> we may still be able to unload it on some
> gullible producer.[9]

It didn't happen. *Time For Elizabeth* was finally put to rest.

We played out of town once more, not with *Time For Elizabeth* but with a version of *You Bet Your Life,* and this time we went to London. In 1964, a young man from Rediffusion TV, a television network now defunct in Britain, approached Groucho to do a program for them. Groucho couldn't resist, asked me to produce the affair, and I insisted on Bernie Smith as a partner. Bernie and I couldn't see Groucho trying out a totally new vehicle at that stage, so we came up with something closely resembling *You Bet Your Life* — a series of comedy interviews with a quiz game to give it focus. It was called *Groucho in Britain* and ran for 13 weeks in 1965.

I can best describe our experience in England by starting with an old joke Groucho told almost every week before the show for 14 years in America. It served a particular purpose. It put the audience on notice that it was okay to laugh at anything they found amusing and that a sophisticated attitude would not serve our purpose or their enjoyment.

> There are all kinds of snobs in the world.
> There are social snobs and financial snobs
> and family snobs. And there are also joke
> snobs. You can tell someone a joke, and if
> they've heard it before, they point a finger
> at you accusingly, as if you were a criminal.
> For example, this is a joke that is at least 50
> years old and that most of you, I'm sure,
> haven't heard. A fat woman walks into a
> drugstore and says to the clerk, "I'd like
> 10 cents worth of chafing powder." The
> druggist says, "Walk this way." And she
> says, "If I could walk that way, I wouldn't
> need the chafing powder."

The joke worked splendidly in Hollywood, but in London it was one of a long list of minor disasters. The truth is, the program simply didn't work in Great Britain. The audiences there obviously expected the glib, crouched-walking Groucho of *Animal Crackers* and *A Night at the Opera.* They were not prepared for the more sedate, sedentary character of *You Bet Your Life* — more Julius than Dr. Hackenbush.

Groucho and Dick Cavett, December 13, 1967 on *Kraft Music Hall's* "A Taste of Funny." (Courtesy Paul Wesolowski)

The chafing powder joke may also give a clue to another reason for our lack of success in Great Britain in 1965. Groucho was baffled when the joke was greeted with general silence from our studio audience in Wembley. He was greatly disturbed when it was explained to him by our British director that it was probably a matter of semantics. It is not a drugstore in Britain, but a pharmacy, and the analgesic is not called chafing powder. It was one of the steps in our gradual realization that, although they seem to speak the same language in England, it is a foreign country. In America, Groucho's familiarity with slang and idiomatic speech allowed him to play with speech patterns, to twist meanings, and probe for hidden clues. In Britain, although he thought he was speaking the mother tongue, he didn't have the lifetime of experience that helps supply all the hidden meanings and innuendoes. Those, after all, were his stock in trade, and he was impoverished without them.

It was no accident that our most successful interview was with an American college student, Phillip Nicholson, from Santa Monica, California. Here, Groucho was right at home again, dealing with the English language as he was used to it, and he and Phillip established immediate rapport.

There were also other differences. Groucho really wasn't dirty enough for them. The standards of propriety on British television were, to our surprise, much looser than in the States. We were interviewed in London by correspondent Robert Musel, and the piece appeared on July 4, 1965, in the *San Francisco Examiner*:

> Robert Dwan, one of Groucho's associates, pulled some slips of paper from his pocket on which he had copied down remarks made on British shows as though to reassure himself he had heard correctly.
>
> "Groucho," he said, "can get pretty racy. He knows all the jokes. But the raciness over here is way beyond him."
>
> "Yes," said Groucho, "but I'm beginning to have quite a time. It's new to me to be able to say anything I want."
>
> "They have a much franker recognition of sex as a fact of life. You can get instant laughter if you start a story with a double meaning. And the funny thing is, unlike the States, the audiences are inclined to consist of women. They laugh the loudest."
>
> "But," commented Dwan, "they won't laugh if the house lights are up. We used to keep them up in the States so Groucho could see the audience. Over here, they

like to do their laughing in the dark, particularly if their minds are way ahead of what Groucho is really saying.

"You should have heard them when Groucho asked a cricket player whether bowling over a maiden in her slip was a bona fide cricket term. They shrieked, even though it is close enough to the real thing."

"The things you can say on television here," Groucho marveled. "We had a young Welsh actress on the other day, and I asked her what she had been doing. She said, 'I was an Indian virgin in a Beatles picture.' I can't imagine an American girl walking up and saying that."

The problems started early. Bernie Smith came over to London several weeks ahead of me. He met me at the plane when I arrived and said, simply, "Go home!"

I wrote to my family in March 1965:

Bernie is encountering all sorts of difficulties in finding contestants. British people don't want to reveal their private lives on the "telly" and it isn't considered comical to have someone prying into their affairs. We've had particular difficulties with members of the upper classes, and especially, of course, with the aristocracy. We did manage to get the noted author, Lady Antonia Fraser, because, I suppose, she had a book to publicize. She was charming and very bright. And we had a certain Lord Hertford, but that was it for the nobles.

As for celebrities, we managed to get the well-known romance writer, Barbara Cartland, flamboyant as always, but, so far, no other notables.

Several members of the staff, including our director, saw four of our old U.S. shows and didn't think they were funny at all.

On June 18, after the first broadcast, I wrote:

> The reviews were exactly what we feared. Worse, really. They said all the things we hoped they wouldn't. Actually, so far, two have been very good, loved it, one has been neutral, and four are violent, just hated the whole thing. They thought it was silly and dull and disgraceful for the great man to be in it. Obviously, they expected Dr. Hackenbush and didn't get him.
>
> I was sitting in a little French coffee shop in Soho at nine a.m. reading the reviews and getting ready to order hemlock, when a very distinguished looking man across the way started telling his friends that he had seen a marvelous program last night, very funny. He started quoting some of the jokes, thought Groucho was wonderful, had great dignity. I went over and thanked him for saving my life.

It is revealing, I suppose, that I didn't save any of the first week's reviews, but the next week I was able to write:

> We've had a couple of more kindly remarks in the press today. *The Observer,* which was particularly nasty the first week, this Sunday says: "I'm delighted to be able to report that the second of the Groucho quiz shows was not only several degrees less excruciating than the first, but in parts quite enjoyable. The frame will always

be crippling, but this time, the veteran anarch, stimulated by a brighter quartet of public stooges, was distinctly more like his chaotic better self. His sparking was still intermittent, but some of his ad lib cracks compared not unfavorably with the Perelman dialogue in *Horse Feathers*."

And the weekly *Spectator* says this week: "The Groucho differed [from other British quiz shows] in the unselfishness with which it encouraged the participants.... A market trader was, in fact, quite as funny as the not-very-funny Master himself. Instead of the usual condescension, Groucho's line was mild aggressiveness and hostility.... Groucho himself, abandoning many of his mannerisms... streamed deadpan wisecracks with a kind of automatism which was sympathetic because it seemed to carry its own self-parody...."

There were a couple of triumphant moments during the British stay. There was a showing of *Animal Crackers* at the British Film Institute, and when Groucho appeared onstage, the audience of students greeted him like a conquering hero with a cheering ovation that lasted at least five minutes.

The other event was a truly impressive occasion, a memorial service for T.S. Eliot involving most of the leading personalities in the London art and theatrical world. Against the background of a 12-foot-tall Henry Moore white sculpture on a huge turntable, we were presented with the Westminster Boys Choir and a Stravinsky Requiem, Peter O'Toole reading "The Love Song of J. Alfred Prufrock," Paul Scofield with some of the quartets, Laurence Olivier reading from *The Waste Land,* Nicol Williamson and a brilliant cast in a musical setting of "Sweeney Agonistes," all very solemn and very much focused on Eliot's preoccupation with death. So the setup was perfect for Groucho to open the second act. Asking Groucho to participate was not as quixotic as it might seem. Groucho and Eliot were friends, mostly by correspondence, but they actually did

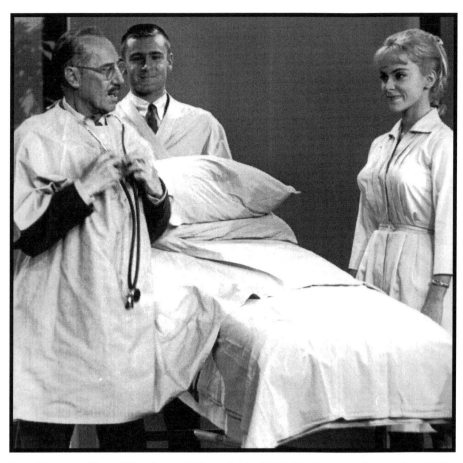

Jack Harmon, Patty Wheeler, and Groucho in *Tell It To Groucho*, September 1962. (Courtesy Paul Wesolowski) For this CBS show which ran one year, we replaced Fenneman with Harmon and Wheeler, which was a mistake. They were bright and attractive, but the Fenneman-Groucho rapport wasn't there. As I recall, the change was made to differentiate the show from *You Bet Your Life*, but it was still an interview/quiz show. Your guess is as good as mine as to what is going on in this publicity photo.

meet in 1964 when Mr. and Mrs. Marx dined with Mr. and Mrs. Eliot at the Eliots' home. The acquaintance began in 1961 with an exchange of autographed photographs and continued on a reasonably regular basis until, and after, their meeting in London.

Groucho wrote to his brother Gummo after the dinner:

> I discovered that Eliot and I had three
> things in common: an affection for good

cigars and cats, and a weakness for making puns.... He is a dear man and a charming host. [10]

When Groucho was introduced at the memorial service, everyone was ready for some comic relief, and when he said, "I never knew what an anachronism was until I was asked to appear here," the response was overwhelming. Then he told an old Vaudeville joke. "I feel like the man who was about to be hanged. He had the noose around his neck and was standing over the trap door when they asked him if he had anything to say. 'Yes,' he said, 'I don't think this damn thing is safe.'"

He then read from Eliot's *Old Possum's Book of Practical Cats,* the poem "Gus the Theatre Cat":

> Gus is the cat at the theatre door.
> His name, as I ought to have told you before,
> Is really Asparagus...
> For he once was a star of the highest degree,
> He has acted with Irving, he's acted with Tree,
> And he likes to relate his success on the Halls
> Where the gallery once gave him seven cat-calls.... [11]

It was a triumph.

(Photofest)

As Long As They're Laughing

CHAPTER 12
Dornum

In the summer of 1958, we had finished the second of our summer tours of *Time For Elizabeth*. *You Bet Your Life* was at its peak, going into its 11th season, and we had our usual 13 weeks off in the summer while the network repeated *The Best of Groucho*. I could juggle the upcoming production schedule to suit Groucho's convenience. He was feeling expansive, so he decided to go to Europe.

It was not a whim, but the fulfillment of a long-standing resolve. When Groucho was very young, his mother, Minnie, had somehow contrived to take him on a visit to her home town, Dornum, in Germany. Now the redoubtable Minnie, the driving force behind the Marx Brothers during the crucial early stages of their career, had become a figure of almost mythic proportions, the heroine of many family stories. It was important to Groucho that his daughter Melinda, then about 12, see the source of that legendary energy, in Dornum.

When Groucho traveled, he demanded comfort. He had slept in too many four-in-a-bed boarding houses, eaten in too many greasy spoon restaurants, to compromise now with quality. He was certainly not a spendthrift. He never conquered the fear that the money might all suddenly disappear. The precarious years of poverty on New York's East Side, and the adventurous but often painful years on the road in Vaudeville were vivid memories.

Groucho, therefore, was not a squanderer. But in the years when he could deal from a position of strength, as a Broadway star, a movie star, and as the indispensable element in a long-running hit TV show, he knew what he wanted and usually got it. When he could stipulate that a limousine or suite at the Astor be provided by the studio, the network, or the sponsor, he did so with glee. He never willingly gave anything away in negotiations with the powerful, but he was often generous to me and others. On this occasion, he invited me and my daughter Judy, then 17, to travel as his guests to Europe with him, his wife Eden, and daughter Melinda.

The burden was eased by our accepting the fruits of a complex deal, arranged through our producer, John Guedel, and realized by Irv Atkins, the genius deal-arranger in the Guedel production office. Somehow, some on-the-air mentions of KLM by Art Linkletter on one of John Guedel's other shows, *People Are Funny*, were transformed into transatlantic air passage for Groucho and party. Thirty-five years later, we still think wistfully of the civilized comfort of the full-sized sleeping berths on that KLM plane.

We flew to Amsterdam and continued our pilgrimage to Minnie's birthplace in a chauffeur-driven limousine, traveling north along the dikes. Groucho sang and taught some of his songs to Melinda and Judy.

One of Groucho's perennial delights was to literalize a cliché. As we traveled across the lowlands, he was not content until we found a spot near a dike suitable for his purpose. We all climbed out of the car and each put a finger in the dike in honor of the heroic little boy in the Dutch legend.

We stopped at a roadside stand, no doubt a spot for our driver to collect a small commission, and all of us, except Groucho, donned traditional Dutch wooden shoes, pantaloons or aprons, and caps. We have the picture to prove it, but not including Groucho. In spite of his own trademark theatrical costume, one of his prime prejudices was against comedians who try to get laughs simply by dressing funny. "Funny hats," was all he needed to say about an act that relied overmuch on props and costumes. He had other capsule critiques. "Elephant doing a toe-dance," referred to an act in which the satisfaction was not from the quality of the performance but from the mere fact that it could be done at all. His most devastating comment was, simply, "Amateur night."

We drove north, then east across the border into Germany and north again along the curve of the North Sea coast through Emden and Norden. Our first sight of Dornum was unexpected. Surrounded by vast flat farm-lands, it was a completely walled village, low brick and stone houses, blank walls turned to the world, not welcoming, silent.

We drove through a gateway, across a narrow cobblestone street, into a large central space, a wide, clean field of hard-packed earth. A wooden church was on a low hill near us, and what looked like a small castle was at the far end.

There were no cars, no bicycles, no people. We walked through a passageway between houses to the cobblestone street. The walls on the street side were mostly blank, broken only by small windows with curtains and a few open doorways. Two children scampered out of sight around a corner. The silence was broken by music—Harry Belafonte singing "The Banana Boat Song."

We found an Inn. Groucho spoke with

Judith Dwan, 16, the author's daughter and Groucho arriving at London's Heathrow airport. A London tabloid ran a story about "Groucho Marx and his teen-age

confidence and fluency in Plattdeutsch, the Low Country dialect that had been used in his home when he was a child. It was a challenge he'd been looking forward to, and he met it to the admiration of his traveling family, and to the delight of the proprietor, who quickly had us seated at a large round table. We were the only customers in the room. Almost immediately, his wife, as large and friendly as the host, appeared from the kitchen with bowls of a most wonderful soup, quickly supplemented by summer sausage, Muenster cheese, black bread, and beer. The friendly but somewhat anxious couple hovered, and as Groucho's command of the language grew more flexible, he easily had them laughing.

"I wonder if they know who you are," Melinda said. Groucho was persuaded to ask them if they knew the Marx Brothers.

"Nein." They had never heard of the Marx Brothers, never seen the movies. A man who had been drinking beer at the bar was now leaning against the door. The Marx Brothers meant nothing to him, either.

Groucho tried to explain. One of the brothers, he said in Plattdeutsch and pantomime, had a mop of red hair and played the harp. Another was a short Italian fellow who played the piano with an orange.

"Nein."

Then Groucho did himself. He put his cigar in his mouth, glided around the room in his crouching lope. They laughed. He wiggled his eyebrows. They laughed again, but did not recognize him.

The food had been excellent, the proprietor and his wife had been friendly, and perhaps there was a small measure of relief for Groucho in not having a reputation to uphold.

A red-haired boy was waiting as we left. Groucho mussed his hair and said something. The boy laughed and ran down the street. The inn-keeper and his wife came to the door and called something to a workman standing across the street. He shouted a question. Groucho pointed to the innkeeper and said, "Braunschweiger!" Laughter followed us down the street as we went toward the castle.

It was, in fact, quite a small castle, but it was built of grayish-brown stone with a few small towers and was encircled by a moat with a draw-bridge. The red-haired boy was waiting with his friends on the wall of the moat. He shouted something. Groucho went over and sat beside him. They spoke in rapid Plattdeutsch, punctuated by much laughter and many gestures from the boys. I could tell from the broad pantomime that they wanted to know about Indians and gangsters. "Chicago!" the red-head said and made the sound effect of a machine gun. He said something funny about Groucho's cigar, Groucho made a joke about his red hair. Sometimes all seven boys were talking at once, but the redhead, clearly the leader, would silence them imperiously while he continued *his* conversation. Finally, a handful of coins from Groucho's pocket sent them all racing off.

Two young women with babies had come out of their houses. A few sentences had them laughing and blushing. They came with us to lead the way to the church. We stayed a long time in the churchyard looking at headstones. Groucho remembered that he had seen the grave of his great grandmother when he had visited the graveyard as a boy. But it was not there now. Finally, we went inside the church with the pastor.

The pastor then showed us the parish register. We assumed that it would have recorded only the Lutheran births in the village, but the Pastor insisted that it was also the official birth register, the only record of the inhabitants of the town. In any case, we found nothing there, as we had found nothing in the graveyard. There was no Minnie Schoenberg in the birth registry, no Schoenberg nor any other Jewish names in the Lutheran graveyard. There was no record of Minnie's life, nor of her mother, Fannie, nor of her father, Lafe, before they left Dornum; no record of any kind of the family who stayed behind. For the record, they had never existed.

The boys were waiting for us outside the church, the red-head in front with a sack of hard candy. The group had grown, and Groucho was quickly surrounded. The rest of us fell behind as they went down the hill, the boys tumbling and scrambling, the red-head marching backward so as not to miss a word.

Groucho's straw hat and cigar did not fit the Pied Piper image exactly, but Hamelin was not far away.

The two young women were waiting at the bottom of the hill with their babies and joined the procession. The innkeeper came along with the workman and three or four others who had come in from the fields. They went with us to the car and Plattdeutsch was mixed with laughter all along the way. The boys ran ahead and trotted alongside the car as we moved slowly off. The red-head took a short-cut and was standing on a mound by the side of the road as we passed. I could see him out of the back window, waving as long as we were in sight.

We drove back to Amsterdam, not saying much, and flew on to Copenhagen. We stayed for two days while the girls and I played in the Tivoli Gardens and Groucho sat on a bench and read the International Edition of the *Herald Tribune*. After Copenhagen, we stopped in Oslo and Frankfurt and, finally, Berlin. West Berlin, even in 1958, was a wonder. My vivid impressions remain of startling new churches of innovative design and of unimaginably delicious pastry at a sidewalk cafe.

Groucho hired a limousine for a trip to East Berlin. It was surprisingly easy. The blockade and airlift had been 10 years earlier, and the Wall was still three years in the future. There was a checkpoint, and the driver, presumably, knew the regulations or the ways around them. We simply drove through a gate into a totally different environment. It seemed that a sepia wash had been applied to the landscape, the buildings, the people. We did not go far into the Zone, but what we saw were vast blocks of identical gray-brown buildings, blank squares of gray-brown earth, and a few people in somber clothing.

The chauffeur's only instruction was to drive us to the bunker where Hitler was said to have died, and where, they said, he was still buried. No guards, no people, no marker, just a pile of rubble, perhaps 20 feet high. Groucho climbed to the top, alone, stood for a moment, and then danced his eccentric, frenetic Charleston. It was not a casual gesture. It went on, maybe for a minute or more. Then he climbed down, we all got in the car and drove back to West Berlin. [1]

CHAPTER 13
The 85th Birthday Party

I didn't see much of Groucho in the later years.

In 1969, Groucho and his wife, Eden, were divorced, and in 1971 Erin Fleming appeared on the scene. Groucho invited me to lunch at Hillcrest Country Club to meet her, telling me in advance that she was "very bright." She was that, but she was also somewhat abrasive. We met on several occasions, and various projects were discussed, but I found that it was not possible to work with her. Groucho told me that he loved her, and I believe that

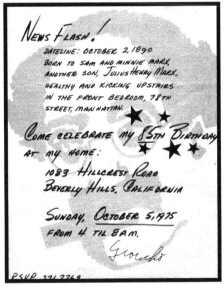

he did. I also believe that she almost literally kept him alive for the last half-dozen years by renewing his interest in life and presenting him with a series of challenging projects, including his triumphant Carnegie Hall Concert. She also apparently made a calculated effort to separate him from his old friends and especially from his family. So, I saw very little of him during those last years.

There was a notable exception on the occasion of his 85th birthday in 1975, when some of the old guard were invited to his house, along with a lot of the new guard. I quote from a letter I wrote to my family:

> George Fenneman was there and John Guedel and Bernie Smith. Groucho's brothers Gummo and Zeppo were there, too, and

Harpo's son, Billy Marx, who played the piano when Groucho sang. Arthur's son Steve was there, but not Arthur nor Miriam nor Melinda. I suppose, although I don't know, that this might be because there was an announcement recently that he is going to adopt the woman who has taken over running his life, Erin Fleming.

Bob Hope was there and made a few remarks, and Milton Berle and Jack Lemmon. There were probably a hundred people, and Groucho sitting quietly in a chair, not smiling, in a loud funny shirt and suspenders. "My children all send greetings," I said. "How are they all?" he said. And then, "I want to sing, but half the people are out there in the patio." And

At Groucho's 85th birthday party: (left to right) Bernie Smith, George Fenneman, Howard Harris and I pose with Groucho. (Frank Diernhammer)

eventually he did sing and half the people stayed out in the patio, the fools, because it was wonderful. Standing very still, with his arms at his sides, and in a very, very, small voice, he sang "Show Me a Rose," "Omaha, Nebraska," "Father's Day," "Ach, How That Woman Could Cook," "Lydia the Tattooed Lady," and "Hooray for Captain Spaulding" and remembered most of the words and hit every one of the notes exactly.

Then, about a half-hour later, Liza Minnelli came in alone and knelt on the floor in front of him as he sang all the songs again just for her. I had the impression that all of the hundreds and hundreds of thousands of people in his audiences over the years had been reduced and concentrated into that one wonderful woman with the adoring gaze.

It was a marvelous moment for what was, almost, his last performance. (He sang one song at a benefit a year later.)

The following Sunday at the University of Southern California was another occasion, offered by the Friends of the USC Libraries in honor of Groucho and the six books he had written. After the program, which featured readings by Jack Lemmon, Lynn Redgrave, Roddy McDowall, and George Fenneman, a member of the audience asked Groucho, "Do you regard yourself as an intellectual?" "No," he said. "I regard myself as a great comedian."

George Fenneman with Groucho at USC's "Lunch with Groucho" benefit, October 1975. (Courtesy Paul Wesolowski)

(Photofest)

As Long As They're Laughing

EPILOGUE

Groucho died on August 19, 1977 at the age of 86.

In New York, we were on the second floor of an office building on Madison Avenue. We had just finished screening some commercials and were on our way to the 32nd floor to pay a courtesy call on a vice-president of the agency. The screening had gone well. No one had quibbled about Groucho's slight deviations from the approved script.

"I would never join a club that would accept me as a member."

This cartoon by Paul Conrad was in *The Los Angeles Times* the morning after Groucho died.

When the elevator arrived from the first floor lobby, it was already almost filled with stony-faced passengers, all attention fixed on the lighted floor signals. As soon as the doors closed, Groucho introduced the silk-bloused executive secretary to the stockbroker standing next to her, assuring them that he would never tell their spouses that he had seen them together. He asked the girl from the typing pool for a date, "...if we can get rid of all these people." They were all laughing when we got off on the 32nd floor. Groucho held the door for a moment, then said, "Now wouldn't this have been a dull trip if I hadn't come along?"

Groucho with his autobiography, which was published in 1959. His dedication reads: "For what it's worth, this book is gratefully dedicated to these six masters without whose wise and witty words my life would have been even duller: Robert Benchley, George S. Kaufman, Ring Lardner, S.J. Perelman, James Thurber, E.B. White. (Photofest)

CHAPTER NOTES

Chapter One

1. *Groucho And Me,* Groucho Marx, Bernard Geis Associates, 1959. Distributed by Random House. p. 90.
2. Ibid., p. 88.
3. George Eels, *Look Magazine*, July 9, 1957.
4. *Hello, I Must Be Going*, Charlotte Chandler, Penguin Books, 1979; Doubleday, 1978, pp. 348-9.
5. *Every Gagwriter's Story,* Dana A. Snow, Copyright 1987 Dana A. Snow, Freedonia Gazette, Vol. 1, Issue 18, Paul Wesolowski, 335 Fieldstone Dr., New Hope, PA 18938-1012 or tfg@cheerful.com.
6. *Love Groucho,* edited by Miriam Marx Allen, Faber & Faber, Boston and London, 1992, pp. 228-9.
7. Ibid., p. 16.
8. Ibid., p. 129.
9. Ibid., p. 30.
10. *Groucho*, Hector Arce, G.P. Putnam's Sons, New York, 1979, p. 263.
11. *Love, Groucho,* p. 98.

Chapter Two

1. *Love, Groucho*, p. 132.
2. Ibid., p. 81.
3. Ibid.
4. Ibid., p. 137.
5. Ibid., p. 142.
6. Ibid., p. 145.
7. *Time*, January 1950.
8. George Eels, *Look Magazine*, July 9, 1957.
9. *Bartlett's Familiar Quotations*, Fourteenth Edition, Little Brown, 1968, p. 1035.
10. *New York Times*, Walter Kerr.
11. *Saturday Review of Literature,* Goodman Ace, October 28, 1950.

A current photo of Groucho's daughter Miriam Marx Allen, editor of *Love, Groucho.*

Chapter Three
1. *Groucho*, Hector Arce, G.P. Putnam's Sons, New York, p. 158.
2. Groucho Marx Archives, The Library of Congress, Washington, DC.

Chapter Four
1. *The Secret Word is Groucho,* Groucho Marx and Hector Arce, G.P. Putnam's Sons, New York, 1976, p. 81.
2. *Time*, December 31, 1951.

Chapter Five
1. *The Fifties*, David Halberstam, Villard Books, New York 1993, p. 272.
2. *The Secret Word is Groucho,* p. 84.
3. Ibid., p. 85.
4. Ibid., p. 85.

Chapter Eight

1. *The Enjoyment of Laughter*, Max Eastman, Simon & Schuster, New York, 1936.

Chapter Nine

1. Groucho Marx Archives, The Library of Congress, Washington, DC, or *The Groucho Letters*, Simon & Schuster, New York, 1967, p. 18.
2. *Love, Groucho*, p. 46.
3. Album, "An Evening with Groucho," A&M Records #SP3515, 1972 Beverly Hills, CA.

Chapter Ten

1. *The Mikado*, Gilbert & Sullivan.

Chapter Eleven

1. *Love, Groucho*, p. 91.
2. Ibid., p. 119.
3. Ibid., p. 95.
4. Ibid., p. 162.
5. Ibid., p. 163.
6. Ibid., p. 165.
7. *The Groucho Letters*, pp. 192-3.
8. *Life With Groucho*, Arthur Marx, Simon & Shuster, 1954, pp. 105-6.
9. *The Groucho Letters*, p. 280, or Groucho Marx Archives, The Library of Congress, Washington, DC.
10. *The Groucho Letters*, p. 164, or Groucho Marx Archives, The Library of Congress, Washington, DC.
11. *Old Possum's Book of Practical Cats*, T.S. Eliot, Harcourt, Brace & Company, 1939, pp. 35-7.

Chapter Twelve

1. A version of this chapter appeared in *The Los Angeles Times*, August 20, 1977, the day after Groucho died.

As Long As They're Laughing

ACKNOWLEDGMENTS

In the preparation of this book, my thanks are due to:

John Guedel for his gift of 20 bound volumes of the original scripts, for a long interview and innumerable telephone calls; beyond that, for his having created *You Bet Your Life* in the first place and for hiring me as director and for having managed to be, at once, a shrewd entrepreneur, a great boss, and a good friend.

George Fenneman for his time, for sharing his memories, and for everything he was to the show.

Buddy Collette for his recollections of the musical side of the program and his help with the Jerry Fielding story.

Eleanor Rowland, our indefatigable show secretary, for having turned out a word-for-word transcript of every one of the 525 programs during those 14 years, and for her recollections of how the show worked.

Miriam Marx Allen for permission to quote extensively from her extraordinary book, *Love, Groucho.*

Susan Dwan Barre for the heroic task of transferring my sometimes legible handwritten manuscript to the computer.

Willis Oborn, my valiant right-hand man during the show years, for his support and recollections.

Paul Schmutz, who supervised the delicate business of keeping the cameras rolling during all those shows and for his memories of how it all worked.

Dorothy Nye, John Guedel's secretary and all-around trouble-shooter, for her help in the very early days.

Roger Rittner, of the Society for the Preservation of Variety Arts, for his help in transferring my ancient acetate recordings to tape.

John and Larry Gassman and their organization, SPERDVAC (Society for the Preservation and Encouragement of Radio Drama Variety and Comedy), for access to their extensive library of broadcast tapes, and to Dan Lippiatt, librarian in the *You Bet Your Life* section of their archives.

Bill Clotworthy for his understanding of the advertising agency role during the BBD&O days and for his anecdotal memory today.

And then there are all the others who made the show work, most of whom are no longer here.

First among these must surely be Bernie Smith, whose words were the base and the raw material for Groucho's creations, and whose skill and judgment in selecting and presenting the contestants was, next to Groucho's, the heart of the show. He was the perfect partner.

Along with Bernie Smith, in the creative department were the writers, Hy Freedman and Howard Harris, and earlier, Dr. Edward Tyler and Elroy Schwartz.

My greatest personal support came from our film editor, Norman Colbert, who managed to cope with our unconventional demands and miles of film that all looked the same to turn out a program a week for 11 years. He also willed to me one of my most valuable resources in writing this book: four reels of out-takes rescued from the cutting-room floor.

There was Hal Lea, of course, who edited the acetate discs at NBC, and Dick Wilson and Molly, later on tape at ABC.

The staff and crew on *You Bet Your Life* were remarkably stable, almost everyone being with us during the whole great collaboration. I remember with gratitude and affection:

Marion Pollock for her impeccable work in researching and writing the quiz and, years later, for allowing me access to her files and her memories.

Eddie Mills, who made a major contribution in discovering and nurturing many of the contestants along with Marion Pollock and his partner, Richard Hall.

Chuck Wohler, our secret weapon, who was the "man in the box" behind the Vizualizer, our cueing device.

Our orchestra leaders, Billy Mills, Stan Meyers, Jerry Fielding, and Jack Meakin, and "the guys in the band": the reeds—Marty Berman, Buddy Collette, Herman Gunkler, and Joey Stabile; the brass—Ralph Fera, Maurie Harris, Seymour Shechlow, and Lloyd Ulyate, later well known as one of the Elliot Brothers; percussionist Tommy Romersa; and Milton Kestenbaum, bass.

Al Borden, the NBC stagehand who, every Wednesday night for 11 years, stood for an hour and a half with his hand on a rigging line ready to drop the duck at the mention of the secret word.

The motion picture crew, provided by the film company, Filmcraft, under the management of Isadore and Regina Lindenbaum and the technical direction of Dr. Ferenz Fodor, who solved all the ridiculous operating problems I threw at him, with head cameramen Jimmy VanTrees, Virgil Miller, and Allan Stensvold; all the cameramen, of whom I especially remember John Finger, whose keen eye brought us a clear, steady close-up of Groucho for 11 years.

The audio engineers, Art Brearley, and Dave Forest.

Bruce Bilson, who labored to put miles of identical-appearing film in synchronization with the sound track, years before he became one of Hollywood's leading TV directors.

Our skillful and speedy makeup artist, Paul Stanhope.

Nate Tufts and Harry Grey of the advertising agency, BBD&O, and Maxine Anderson of the agency for Toni, whose not inconsiderable job was to interpret the idiosyncrasies of Mr. Marx to the clients.

Norman Frisch, the NBC publicity man who kept us in the public eye.

Dick Dwan, my brother, who was my assistant before he joined BBD&O.

Melinda Marx, who performed so dutifully and so well, if sometimes reluctantly, in her annual guest appearances as singer and dancer, and for bringing with her, one year, the guest star I remember best, appearing with her father (without Charlie McCarthy), the beautiful teenage Candice Bergen.

And, finally, the one who was the heart and soul of the whole enter-prise, the one, the only, Groucho.

BIBLIOGRAPHY

Adamson, Joe, *Groucho, Harpo, Chico and Sometimes Zeppo,* Simon & Schuster, NY, 1973.

Allen, Miriam Marx, *Love, Groucho,* Faber & Faber, Boston, 1992.

Anobile, Richard, *The Marx Bros. Scrapbook,* Darien House, 1973.

Arce, Hector, *Groucho,* G.P. Putnam's Sons, NY, 1979.

Barson, Michael, ed., *Flywheel, Shyster & Flywheel,* Pantheon Books, NY, 1988.

Chandler, Charlotte, *Hello, I Must Be Going,* Doubleday & Company, NY, 1978.

Crichton, Kyle, *The Marx Brothers,* Doubleday & Company, Garden City, NY, 1950.

Eastman, Max, *Enjoyment of Laughter,* Simon & Schuster, NY, 1948.

Halberstam, David, *The Fifties,* Villard Books, NY, 1993.

Marx, Arthur, *Life With Groucho,* Simon & Schuster, NY, 1954.

Marx, Groucho, with Hector Arce, *The Secret Word is Groucho,* G.P. Putnam's Sons, NY, 1976.

Marx, Groucho, *The Groucho Letters,* Simon & Schuster, NY, 1967.

Marx, Groucho, *Groucho & Me,* Bernard Geis Associates, 1963.

Marx, Groucho, *Memoirs of a Mangy Lover,* Bernard Geis Associates, 1963.

Marx, Harpo, with Rowland Barber, *Harpo Speaks,* Bernard Geis Associates, 1961.

Wesolowski, Paul, *The Freedonia Gazette,* 1981-1989, Paul Wesolowski Publisher, New Hope, PA.

ABOUT THE AUTHOR

Robert Dwan was born in San Francisco, grew up in Burlingame, California, attended Stanford University, from where he graduated in 1935. He worked in radio from 1936 as a writer/director in San Francisco and Hollywood, covering such shows as *Red Skelton* and *Fibber McGee & Molly*. He was staff writer for *People Are Funny* for seven years. He directed *You Bet Your Life* for its entire run on radio and television from 1947 to 1961. Recently, he taught classes on comedy at the University of Southern California. His wife, Lois Dwan, was restaurant critic and columnist for the Los Angeles Times. They have three sons, two daughters and seven grandchildren and live in Santa Monica, California.

INDEX

**If you enjoyed this book,
call or write for a free catalog
Midnight
Marquee Press
9721 Britinay Lane
Baltimore, MD 21234**

**410-665-1198
www.midmar.com**

Made in the USA
Middletown, DE
15 January 2015